D1526700

A COMFORTABLE RANGE

A Hunter,

His Bird Dog,

And Their Quest For

A COMFORTABLE RANGE

By Jim McDermott

COUNTRYSPORT PRESS
CAMDEN, MAINE

ISBN 0-89272-675-X
Library of Congress Control Number: 2004116482

Printed at Versa Press Inc., East Peoria, Illinois

5   4   3   2   1

Countrysport Press
P.O. Box 679
Camden, ME 04843
A division of Down East Enterprise Inc., publishers of *Shooting
Sportsman* magazine, www.shootingsportsman.com

For book orders and catalog information, call 800-685-7962,
or visit www.countrysportpress.com

For Liz

CONTENTS

ACKNOWLEDGMENTS

PROLOGUE

HOUSEBOUND 19

RANGING WEST 35

MINNESOTA: RUFFED GROUSE 49

SOUTH DAKOTA: PRAIRIE GROUSE 71

SOUTH DAKOTA: RING-NECKED PHEASANTS, PART I 99

SOUTH DAKOTA: RING-NECKED PHEASANTS, PART II ... 125

EPILOGUE 151

ACKNOWLEDGMENTS

For welcoming itinerant Easterners time after time, and for teaching us more than a thing or two, my sincere thanks go out to family in South Dakota and Minnesota. I'd also like to express my gratitude to Clarence, Randy, and Gary for their good humor and remarkable generosity to out-of-towners. Countless people have been kind enough to take me hunting, and I thank them all, especially John the Fish-Slayer, B-Paw, and Uncle Jim. I'd like to say thank you to Dick and Cousin Michael, Trevor, Andrew, and Jack and Paul as well. Much-needed support during the trip was provided by the Grouse Camp crew, particularly the Olson brothers; by Walter and Michael; and by the Duluth physician who told stories on the grass-lands about his wild Llewellins. I'm also indebted to the Cottonwood Lake Resort, Taylor's Steakhouse, La Minestra, and the Jefferson Debating Society. For unerring guidance in editorial matters, I would like to thank Chris Cornell and especially Joe Arnette. Most of all, I'm grateful to my parents and to my siblings and their families, for love and encouragement, and to my dear wife for getting mixed up in this bird dog world with me.

The more I got on, the more I felt that, really, one can find something only in that way—in the same way in which, say, a dog runs through a field. If you look at a dog following the advice of his nose, he traverses a patch of land in a completely unplottable manner. And he invariably finds what he is looking for.

—W.G. Sebald, an interview

PROLOGUE

Dogs, like men, lose their range and enthusiasm for
life from having the wildness in them questioned.
—Guy de la Valdene, *For a Handful of Feathers*

I named him in honor of an English setter, presum-
ably a Laverack type, once owned by sporting writer
George Bird Evans, but, as a Llewellin, Speck didn't
much resemble one of Evans's graceful, home-bred
Old Hemlock giants with equine heads, pendulous
jowls, and huge feet. Tall and skinny, Speck weighed,
at most, forty-five pounds in the off-season, just thirty-
nine when he'd been hunting prairie grouse and ring-
necked pheasants for a month straight. In November,
after grass and brush had beaten the wispy feathering
from his chest and legs, his spare, angular body suggested an abstract drawing of a universal setter, not
unlike the austere sketches that illustrate Evans's
books.

Speck's white body was marked everywhere with
irregular black shapes that often touched; his muzzle,

legs, and paws were ticked with dozens of tiny brown spots. His eyelashes were white, and a pair of black quotation mark shapes was prominent between his brown eyes—eyes that reflected an otherworldly intelligence.

As a tricolor instead of an orange or blue belton, he probably should have had at least one eye patch, an oval shadow that bled into the black fur of one ear, introducing a hint of comical menace to his face. I wanted my third setter to be his own dog, however, rather than an image of Remington or Huckleberry, Speck's predecessors who were also tricolor Llewellins, so I held out through several litters for a rare patchless male.

Although it was impossible not to see in Speck the ghosts of dogs I once knew and still loved, his unblemished eyes functioned in another way: they visibly signified how special he was, how strange and wonderful he seemed to me, as much for the things he wouldn't do as for the things he would.

Above all else, there was the matter of range; that is, the distance at which a bird dog quarters in front of a hunter, the space he puts, at any given moment, between himself and the gun during his search for game. Generations of Speck's forebears had been selectively bred for foot-hunting traits: they had moved with exquisite deliberation before the gun, keeping in contact with the hunter who went on foot through small, thick coverts rather than on horseback through open fields.

As it happened, though, Speck was unlike his ancestors in an important way—his natural range had no limit other than a point. Like the stereotypical big-running field-trial pointer, he would quarter at top speed and never let up until a bird stopped him.

In my neurotic imagination, the field held any number of threats to the well-being of a bird dog— rattlesnakes, thin ice, road traffic, guns, traps, porcupines, rabid skunks, heat stroke, hypoglycemia, holes, bad water, rotten flesh, swift currents, barbed wire, even shards of glass—but when hunting with Speck I most feared his push for the excessive range that led to loss.

How could I prevent a bird dog who displayed so much drive from becoming lost forever? How could I keep Speck from straying for just long enough to wander across a deadly highway or into the front yard of a landowner who shot "stray dogs" on sight?

I wanted to keep Speck safe and, at the same time, I wanted to have the pleasure of watching him run, but it wasn't easy to figure out how to do these things without diminishing his enthusiasm for our time in the uplands. Learning to hunt with Speck in an authentic way meant learning not to question the wildness in him, as Guy de la Valdene so rightly puts it. More than anything else, that learning was what our quest for a comfortable range was all about.

HOUSEBOUND

There was a man and a dog too this time.
—William Faulkner, "The Bear"

Speck arrived in the summer of 1996 by plane from a small Southern city. Crouched inside a plastic crate that had been set down on a loading dock at Washington National Airport, he was a tiny speckled creature staring out at the uniformed passersby and rolling forklifts. I snatched him up in my arms and took him home to our suburban Arlington, Virginia, neighborhood a few miles away.

On the domestic side of our daily existence, I treated Speck, from the start of our time together, as house pets were treated, but he refused for the most part to become one. He barked maniacally at the sight of dogs being walked past the house, but he also responded at the top of his lungs to faint birdsong and to the voices of small children walking to school. On hearing the slightest noise, he raced up the hallway and began furiously clawing at the front door. An alien scent that had drifted in through a gap where a window met its frame triggered barking and sprinting after entities that never materialized except in his imagination. On the whole, he did not seem to notice, even as a puppy, that there were walls dividing his home from the outside world, that his everyday territory had limits.

Speck would greet me at the door with vigorous swipes of his tail that caused his entire body to wag as he showed off a plush doughnut or rope-limbed monkey. I thought that a human being could never seem so happy and remain sincere. He begged for treats by resting his snout as heavily as he could on my leg while whimpering more and more insistently, and with increasing volume and rising pitch, until he was almost screaming with impatience. He ate his lamb-and-rice chow only after midnight, loudly and with liberal use of water. If I tossed a cracker in his direction, he would vault into a wild leap, as though he'd been stung by a bee, and the cracker would hit him in the chest. Basement crickets he stalked, pointed, and killed with sharp slaps of his front paws, then rolled on them. Sometimes he ate the crickets, shaking his head and gagging at the taste. He rubbed his snout pleasurably on the couch cushions downstairs but, with his usual sensitivity to where he was, he never jumped on the nice furniture in the living room.

As the months went by, Speck learned to follow me around the house in case I decided to take him out for training or hunting rather than grade papers for a class I was teaching or work on my half-finished doctoral dissertation about minimalist writing. He became highly skilled at anticipating my fits of pro-crastination—before I could switch off the computer and pick up the car keys, he headed directly to the back door and began to whimper. He liked to howl musically, with his head thrown back, when some-thing delighted him, such as the sound of my older brother John's truck idling in the driveway (a sound that I, too, associated with hunting trips). At night he irritated a chronic, dime-sized lick granuloma on his foot and stuck whole paws into his mouth and chewed his claws. Because he always tried to be where I was, doing what I was doing, he often fell asleep on the bed at night, but as soon as I moved the slightest bit he leaped to the floor and circled, then curled up and sighed dramatically. He liked to walk up to me as I sat reading and violently throw his body back first upon my shoes. When Speck growled at me for touching his flank the wrong way, I grabbed his muzzle, took him down, and sat on him while pre-tending to bite his ears. But I suspected that this tactic, which I had read about in a magazine article on dominance-aggression complex, merely amused him, causing him to show aggression more often in attempts to bait me into play.

By the end of our second season together, those who had seen Speck hunt had judged him to be an unusually fine bird dog, which made it even easier for me to brag about him. His athletic ability was such that, when the mood inexplicably struck him, he could leap on top of a picnic table from a standing position. One of his gaits was an effortless glide during which no part of him seemed to move except for his legs. Another was a series of graceful, reaching jumps that he strung endlessly together when negotiating thick grass that was higher than his head or when descending a severely sloped hillside. Still another was a low-to-the-ground sprint in which his back legs kicked high and his front legs were regularly parallel to the ground. Whichever gait he happened to be using, he hunted at a blistering pace all day, displaying, at every instant, more style than Llewellins are supposed to have: a high head and tail, a lean body that remained upright and unmoving through hard turns to follow scent, an ability to float through grass in a manner that seemed to defy gravity.

In the way he pointed, Speck gave an impression of coiled, feral energy, as though to touch him would have provoked a whirling attack, as though he needed to kill the pointed bird to stay alive. Behind this intensity was a fine nose honed by sustained exposure to wild birds.

One windy afternoon on the short-grass prairie in South Dakota, where we hunted for several weeks each year, he locked up in a flat expanse that spread out for hundreds of yards beneath a steep, square hill. I stomped around to the front—nothing. We played this birdless game several times, with Speck's finds pulling me first into the shadow of the hill, then up it. Finally, at the crest, we discovered a large flock of sharptails, which he pointed with his typical intensity. After the birds had outwitted me, I glanced down to where he had first pointed them and imagined how tiny we would have looked when he initially made game and realized that these sharptails were out there. On other days, he trailed scores of spooky pheasants through South Dakota's vast public hunting areas and pinned them in undifferentiated seas of hot grass. The ability to pin pheasants evidenced not simply a good nose but also bird sense, and Speck clearly had a knack for empathizing with those sprinting roosters until he knew them better than they knew themselves. Sometimes I suspected that he wanted to become one.

For all of these reasons, I assumed that Speck was the most gifted bird dog I would ever own, and I was deeply grateful for my good luck. However, the headlong drive that made him a raw genius in the field was a cause for concern as much as for giving thanks: I feared that some day he would range so far ahead of me that I would be left behind forever.

. . .

Speck's pure aggressiveness in the field had always resembled a small-scale miracle because it was so strange to behold in a dog from his bloodline. Accordingly, when he no longer seemed to be all puppy, I began a lengthy effort to reduce his range without diminishing his unexpectedly wild and glorious desire to reach out and find birds. As my training notebook sometimes read after Speck turned eight months old: "How to control him the right way?"

It soon became obvious that Speck was unlike bird dogs who naturally stuck close to handlers out of insecurity or out of a quasi-human regard for their masters' company. I learned this fact by performing a series of experiments described by a famed gun-dog trainer. The trainer suggests that you take your young dog out for a romp, then hide behind a tree. The dog realizes that he can no longer see you, becomes anxious, and makes a beeline for where you used to be standing. By doing this regularly, you teach your dog always to take your position into account as he works cover; thus, he learns to hunt with you. But Speck did not come back to get me. In fact, he did not even glance in my direction. From my post behind trees, I usually could discern a splendid burst of acceleration provoked by a scattering flock of mourning doves or a gust of wind. Fair enough: I decided that it was better for Speck to hunt for birds than to hunt for me.

Alternatively, some trainers reduced speed and range by attaching awkward devices to a collar—heavy plastic balls, log chains, two-by-fours—that impaired the dog's ability to run. Assuming a strong desire to search for birds, these trainers addressed the dog's body alone, interfering with and, in a sense, disabling his physical capacity. Other people used check cords that were never meant to be removed, even going so far as to hunt with these leads secured to their waists. Like sled dogs, their setters did the thankless work of tugging them forward through the woods. But these and the other coercive methods I had heard about were similarly flawed. Each would have prevented Speck from learning what it was like to make his own choices in the field acting on what his nose and his innate bird sense were telling him about how to make game. Consequently, he would not have had even a fighting chance to become the strange genius that he was born to become.

I tried to remember how my brother and I had

kept our first setter, Remington, close. A burly Llewellin, Rem had been the family dog, and John and I, being energetic kids obsessed with the original *Gun Dog* magazine, had done our best to train him. A basement Ping-Pong table had been the scene of innumerable Whoa and Fetch lessons, and we had planted pigeons for Rem to find on the soccer fields of a middle school located behind the house in which we grew up. The birds flew back to a spacious plywood-and-wire coop my brother had built on the porch roof or were reclaimed after short flights hauling pieces of garden hose (as tennis players or cross-country teams looked on with perplexity and alarm). Once John had a driver's license, we began to road-trip throughout Virginia and West Virginia on fall weekends in search of moments complete with a pointing Llewellin setter, crumbling stone walls, fire-red maples, and wheeling ruffed grouse.

At some point, it occurred to me that if we simply let Rem run around for an hour—no matter how old he was—he would reliably settle down to hunt with the Llewellin's typical thoroughness and cool. But Speck's blood ran hot by comparison with Remington's; an hour of free running was not enough to reduce his range. Six hours of scrambling over boulders and launching himself through wild grape tangles in the West Virginia grouse woods did have a slight effect, but it made no sense to spend more time tiring Speck out than hunting. And what was the difference anyway?

Although vigorous exercise was not the answer, reining Speck in with a few commands was, at least to a degree. When he had reached what I saw as the outer limits of an acceptable range for the cover and the type of bird we were hunting—as much as half a mile on the short grass prairie during a sharptail hunt—I would blow the whistle twice, which he understood to mean Here based on untold repetitions at the end of a check cord. To make things clear even at the greatest distances, I used the loudest whistle I could find and backed up the command using an electronic collar with a one-mile range. Next, when Speck had come in part of the way, I blew the whistle once for Change direction and used a hand signal to indicate which direction and to widen his first cast. Last, to keep him quartering in a tight pattern ahead of the gun, I continually gave the Change-direction command. A pragmatic way of imposing range, this technique was similar to an approach described by gun-dog authority Jerome Robinson. Proving its value over time, the technique enabled us to grow into a fairly efficient bird-getting team.

But something was wrong with hunting this way. Although Speck usually obeyed the many commands

I was throwing at him, he did not accept the idea behind them in the absence of nonstop coercion. For three seasons and off-seasons we marched forward in a hail of earsplitting noise, with the obedient bird dog precisely navigating the cover in response to the nit-picking demands of his control-freak handler. Every few seconds in the ruffed grouse woods and slightly less often in pheasant country's tall grass, a command was there to be obeyed or to be enforced. It was as if we had given up real hunting in order to perform a stylized ritual governed by precise measurements. As our experiences afield grew increasingly artificial and inauthentic, both of us, it seemed, began to wish for a way to become more attuned to the hunt. Yet when the whistle fell silent and the hand signals stopped, Speck would adopt his natural range once more. It was the return of what had been repressed, another bit of evidence telling me that the awesome drive in Speck's heart was stronger than my poor ability to teach him what he needed to know. I respected his attachment to an experience with which he was obsessed (to run big), and I appreciated his willingness to cooperate with me in my own obsession (to hack him back in). But I couldn't help worrying each time he seemed to be on the brink of disappearing, at the edge of being just out of reach. And I couldn't stop myself from blowing the whistle.

Sometimes, however, we glimpsed a different kind of experience, one in which a tacit understanding between Speck and me allowed self-forgetfulness to take over. Usually we were in South Dakota when it happened, in some vast, empty place full of grass, following a running pheasant or tracking a flock of sharptails. We would find ourselves dropping down into the chase and losing track of our respective obligations to blow the whistle and swing around to the front, and we would simply pursue the birds as best we could, so as to find and kill them. During these times, Speck hunted at just the right distance from me without having to be forced to do so, and I allowed the silence around us to build rather than filling the air with commands.

I don't know what Speck felt at such times, but for me it was like being lost in the most fascinating book in the world, a book that refused to stop unfolding and that you were reading and writing at the same time. The older Speck got, the more our hunting became, for me, a quest to experience these privileged but elusive moments of absorption and forgetting.

• • •

My fear that I would lose Speck for good proved to be unwarranted during three solid years of hunting and training. However, he had been lost temporarily perhaps half a dozen times, and I tended to dwell on those experiences. One of the worst days I still remember very well.

Speck was about ten months old. We were doing some off-season training in a timber tract in rural Virginia, not far from where we lived then. For the first thirty minutes of work, Speck had fought the check cord, his exasperated body thrashing around like a hooked fish. Worn down by frustration and by the force of the rope tearing into my knuckles, I decided to let him drag the check cord.

White in the dusky light, Speck descended the long hill before us at a dead sprint. Pivoting sharply to stay on the trail, he tore the soft ground apart, splashing the bushes at the base of the hill with flecks of mud. It was a stirring display of speed and grace that driven bird dogs are capable of.

In the distance, I could hear a dog bark halfheart- edly, as if attempting to have the last word in an argument with his master, but Speck had become as silent as a cloud drifting through the evening sky.

A wet snow began to fall. Speck was out there opening up a great distance between us, with no thought in his mind except to find birds as quickly as possible or to run as far as the impulse would take him. Yet there was almost nothing for him to dis- cover: the woods were devoid of life save for a few emaciated white-tailed deer. Then again, perhaps he had decided to chase whitetails. Rounding a bend in the trail, I was surprised at how poorly my eyes were adjusting to what had suddenly become darkness. The woods were silent until I finally used the whistle.

For hours I searched the same ground over and over again in the snow. I drove to farms and blew the whistle over the heads of cattle, trespassed, and knocked on doors. A skinny, bearded man dressed in workclothes and a bathrobe answered one door. The house behind him was dark and smelled of cooked cabbage. I had never seen this man before—I had heard that he and his wife were artists—yet I wanted to ask or even beg him to perform a miracle, to conjure Speck the way he conjured the beings supposedly depicted in his paintings. In the end, he shuffled backward in his slippers and slammed the door in my face.

At midnight, I got the car stuck outside a run-down mansion surrounded by acres of woods and pasture. By gunning the engine I freed the tires but left deep ruts in the yard and a spray of red mud on the front walk.

As I drove too fast down a curving, hilly road on my way to search another patch of land, the headlights caught arcs of green woods careening by. I tried to convince myself that Speck was about to materialize in one of those illuminated spaces.

By 2 A.M. I was back home. I feared that Speck's check cord had become tangled in brush and that he would slowly starve, or that he had been struck by a car and was already dead. As I tried to explain these fears during a phone call to my brother John, I found myself, in my exhaustion and worry, barely able to speak.

At 3 A.M. I heard claws clicking on the porch. I grabbed Speck's collar, pulled him inside, and hugged him. I dried him with a towel and brought food and water. He gorged himself for several minutes before collapsing into a sleep that continued into the next afternoon.

Thinking back upon why Speck might have run off, it occurred to me that there had been a glistening coldness in his eyes as I released the check cord, that his movements had become so fluid they appeared to be unconscious when he moved away from me, as though he had fallen into a dream. What was in his mind, I wondered, during that monumental run?

For several months after that night, I never dropped my new one-hundred-foot-long check cord—custom-ordered because of its absurd length— and whenever I exchanged it for the leash I kept a tight grip on Speck's collar. This was not exactly rational behavior, but I caught myself thinking, again and again, of what we had found during a past bird hunt far from home.

At the end of a cold November day, Speck had stopped and looked questioningly at a stand of tall grass. There was a dead Brittany inside, and it had no collar. It had been struck by a car on the gravel road fifty yards away, I thought, and had crawled into the grass to die. At the motel where we were staying I tried to contact the local game warden but finally gave up—he was never home—and fell asleep.

For weeks thereafter I had intended to report what had happened, but I never did. I had wanted to let someone know that the bird dog they had been looking for had finally been found and there could be an end to wondering.

RANGING WEST

Yea, a great . . . dog comes too seldom and is too
valuable when he does appear, to be toyed with.
—William Harnden Foster,
New England Grouse Shooting

It was early in the summer of 1999, about three
months before my annual Midwest hunting trip. I sat
down in the living room one night to lace up my running shoes, thinking that it was time for both me and
Speck, who lay on the floor beside the piano, to work
off some recent high-calorie indulgences. In honor of
his third birthday, I had presented him with a grilled
New York strip steak on a clean plate while granting
myself—on the thinnest of pretexts—the boon of a
twenty-ounce rib eye with a Guinness or two to wash
it down. Gift-wrapped tins of dog biscuits for Speck,
along with the odd bag of jellybeans for me and my
hopeless sweet tooth, had arrived by mail courtesy
of family members, so we had plenty of work to do,

perhaps four miles in heat and humidity that would take a toll even at 10 P.M.

My aim was to be as unencumbered and swift as an acquaintance of mine—a rail-thin, long-legged gentleman lawyer and pointer enthusiast who, at sixty years of age, was still flying up and down the steepest ridges that made his beloved ruffed grouse coverts daunting terrain indeed; even in sprawling quail country this man had no need of a horse because he himself had become so much like one. By doing what I could to keep up with Speck, I intended to let him push the envelope of range in South Dakota, especially, while we worked at drawing the boundaries together.

"Let's go," I said, and stood up. Eyeing me, Speck stretched himself more fully across the carpet. I walked to the front door and said, "Want to go outside?" Uttered in the ritual way, these words triggered something preconscious and caused Speck's ears to twitch. But even when I had pulled the door open there was no response other than a sleepy groan and more stretching. Speck opened and closed his front paws with deliberation and slowly shut his eyes.

Normally he demanded to come along on these regular workouts, after which he would be as fresh as he had been a few miles before while being less agitated by things he heard or saw. The jogs supplemented the check-cord training and conditioning we had done in the relatively cool mornings.

It turned out that Speck wasn't sick; he was just smart. For obvious reasons, he had sworn off running on hot concrete in the summer. And so, beginning the next day and continuing until September when we left for Minnesota ruffed grouse cover, the surplus energy that he would have expended on our suburban sidewalks was channeled more frantically than ever before into warning Scottish terriers and the mailman to get away from the front yard, and otherwise into investing the mundane occurrences of our domestic life with faint predatory resemblances to hunting.

Speck's behavior that summer was not literally destructive, but it was profoundly distracting. The reason I allowed him to be so wild, I think—and he became more and more so the closer it got to our September departure—was that I understood and identified with his behavior. Living in a state of anxiety that confounded reason and discipline, desperate to head west and start the new season, both of us, in our own ways, knew that we would feel better in the field than we did in the house.

• • •

Although I'd set aside two days to get ready, I was up late the night before Speck and I were to leave on our trip to the Midwest. By shuffling my schedule and taking on extra work the preceding winter, spring, and summer, I had freed up the fall for hunting while generating the income to finance our longest expedition yet—about six weeks of hunting public land, eating grocery store meals, and staying with relatives or in mom-and-pop motels that charged twenty-five dollars a night. Sometimes, when even these measures seemed too wasteful, we would live out of the truck instead.

As Speck rested on the basement couch, his white, curled feathering spilling across the blue cushions, I spread gear over the carpet and began putting things into duffel bags. There was a bag, for instance, to contain the few pieces of important bird-dog equipment I had culled from all that I owned. Within a tangle of grass-stained check cords and muddy harnesses and frayed lanyards holding several generations of Acme Thunderers were a long-range electronic collar, Speck's very favorite brush—actually some sort of German horse comb—and a still-white retrieving dummy that had been stalked and subdued many times but rarely brought to hand.

Into another bag I crammed such things as a Gore-Tex parka (faded, stained with pheasant blood, and no longer waterproof), two pairs of threadbare field pants, and a vest that ejected pine needles, dirt, pulverized leaves, and feathers whenever I picked it up.

Greasy nickels and Milk-Bone crumbs fell out, too. There were many more bags to fill.

I wandered out into the rain to load the truck. When I had finished, I realized that, with the exception of a sock wedged inside a gun case, I'd forgotten to pack any regular clothes. None of the duffel bags were left, but, after sorting through my closet for ten minutes, I was able to stuff a plastic trash bag with enough clothes to last two weeks without a wash.

I set the alarm for 5:30 A.M. and got in bed. Although Speck slept contentedly, nerves kept me awake for an hour. Irritated by what novelist Henry James terms "the imagination for disaster," I was feeling certain that Speck would vanish or that our trip would be marred by a lesser calamity. My fears were undoubtedly even more irrational than usual owing to something I had found earlier in the day.

While getting some of Speck's veterinary records in order for the trip, I had run across and been unable to prevent myself from opening, for the first time in years, my Huckleberry file, which contained all sorts of documents about my second Llewellin.

Huck was just five months old when he suddenly fell ill—at least, it seemed sudden to me. One afternoon he began to cough quietly, but, as it turned out, he had been sick for weeks or months, and sick with such stealth that his regular veterinarian, who had examined him just the day before, had failed to see a hint of illness. At an emergency veterinary hospital, Huck was found to have fluid in his lungs—pulmonary edema—because of a dysfunctional heart valve that had caused a series of minor and undetectable but ultimately fatal heart attacks.

Three days following the initial emergency, after taking Huck to several veterinarians, including a canine cardiologist at a well-equipped referral hospital, I decided to have my setter pup (who was by then in intensive care) put to sleep. The last thing I remember is that he stood up on wobbly legs and walked over to meet me at the door of the strange little chamber in which they had placed him, and that he put his head in my hands so that I could rub the soft, almost silky fur beneath his chin.

Huck had been a sweet-natured little fellow who seemed old and therefore wise before his time, partly, I think, because his body had been a malfunctioning, perhaps burdensome thing that weighed him down, attracting him to stillness and rest. I wept on the day he died. And soon I was writing down some thoughts that I found myself reading again nearly five years later:

In the basement are the pieces necessary to build a training table; the week he died, Huck was to begin his Whoa training with all the amenities. I was to fashion the sawhorses, sheets of plywood, and hinges into his plaything, and he was to pace it like a library lion come to life. I have the plans for a better pigeon coop in my briefcase, and some notes about training schedules, and a barely begun training notebook with lots of exclamation points in it. Sometimes I put my hand into a pocket of the parka Huck had muddied daily with his paws, and I find biscuits there but never want to take them out, because I cannot give them to him. I have had to imagine a future that will never be in order to give Huck the life he will never have. These are not memories at all so they are perfect, or I change them.

My first impulse was to view the writer of this as someone I no longer was, someone more sentimental, I guess, and less hard-boiled. But this impulse did not last, and I reminded myself that I was still one of the world's biggest suckers for bird dogs, a person liable to get choked up just listening to a story about some little bird dog puppy who had pointed a grouse wing.

I paged through the other documents, including the results of biopsies done by the University of

Pennsylvania and a private veterinary research facility in New York, but I still had no answer to this question: What killed Huck by destroying his heart? Parvovirus was not responsible. It might have been a congenital cardiac muscle flaw or a metabolic disorder, or even a virus that had yet to be named, but no one knew. The veterinarians remarked that they had never seen a heart so rickety in a dog so young (and Huck came from sound genetic stock); they found the difficulty in explaining his death frustrating, and so did I.

When Huck's retrieving dummy was not much smaller than he was and had to be half-dragged, he would bring it to hand eagerly. His overpowering need to retrieve turned up rough treasures such as pencils, pop cans, and golf balls. There are few sights more endearing than a setter pup trotting past in high-tailed style with an apron or a huge flower or a tattered sports section in his mouth. So, as I tried once more to fall asleep—it was nearly 4 A.M. at this point—I imagined Huckleberry in the act of giving me, over and over again, some humble object. Soon I was no longer fretting about cartoon images of striking rattlesnakes, embodiments of my fear that, out in the field one day, something unlucky was going to happen to Speck and thus to me as well.

. . .

I awoke at 10 A.M. the next day, which was September 15. There was no reason to believe that the alarm had ever sounded. For an hour I took care of last-minute details, which chiefly meant rounding up unpaid bills, highway maps, and books related to my halting academic research. My sense as I finally backed the truck down the driveway was that I had left something very important behind, most likely a scrap of paper on which a telephone number was written. During the drive through Arlington, I thought of the way Speck had sprinted to the tailgate and leaped directly into his crate. Two other seasons that had begun with journeys west had taught him to wait for this day.

It was raining so hard on Route 66 out of northern Virginia that cars were pulling off onto the road's shoulder. I pushed past them in my old truck, which had over two hundred thousand miles on the odometer and smelled like wet Llewellin all the time but showed relatively few signs of imminent collapse. Still fighting a heavy rain and gusting winds (the remnants of Hurricane Dennis) we made bad time on Route 29 to Charlottesville, Virginia, reaching a connector road to Interstate 64 after 2 P.M.

Stopped at another light in town, I began to question my decision to take the southern route to Iowa before turning toward St. Paul, Minnesota, where my mother's twin brother, Jim, was waiting for us; with the ease of rural interstate came the struggle of at least two hundred additional miles. I had misgivings, too, because I knew Charlottesville well—it was the home of the University of Virginia, from which I hoped to earn my doctorate—and it seemed oddly charming under these conditions. In the crosswalk I could see, through the streaked windshield, a crowd of umbrella-toting students migrating to the English department. The image made me want to leave the road and seek shelter in the library, where the stacks would have smelled wonderfully of book dust, and I would have had the pleasure of lifting my head from my reading and looking out at the dismal weather.

I bought gas at the edge of campus instead, and I took Speck for a five-minute walk in the rain. He strained at the leash, chasing a scent and, perhaps, wondering if it were already time to go hunting.

The fog was suddenly thicker on Afton Mountain as I switched from drowsing public radio classical music to a recording of a novel that involved bird hunting. The protagonist, an elderly man suffering from terminal cancer, intended to take his Brittanies out for a final bird hunt on the sagelands. I stopped listening for a time. When I chose to concentrate on the novel again, it seemed to register undertones of condemnation, or maybe just regret, about the killing of birds.

The ethics of hunting was, of course, a popular subject. There were numerous books and even some pedagogical videotapes devoted to sport hunting's justification. The outdoor magazines constantly revisited the subject, giving advice, for example, on how to win a "dinner party argument," whatever that was, with someone who opposed hunting. For my part, I had stopped trying to justify my hunting. For example, I couldn't say—at least not with a straight face—that I hunted because nature compelled me as a predator to kill to survive. Despite the predator-like position of my eyes and the indisputable fact of man's privileged position in the food chain, it obviously wasn't necessary for me to prey upon animals to avoid death. I didn't hunt because I had to; I hunted because I wanted to. Nor did I hunt because doing so kept wildlife populations strong and saved wilderness by funding conservation. These were extremely valuable consequences but not justifications that I would have pointed to.

We must do all sorts of things simply because by doing them we avoid becoming strangers to ourselves, and hunting birds with Speck seemed to belong to me so much that I would not have been the same person without him. He was mysteriously instrumental in preserving almost the only part of me that I could bear to appreciate, which I thought of as my fragile ability not to go dead inside despite constant pressure to do just that. I had built my life around Speck because I wanted to keep this piece of myself going, and I felt no further need to justify the hunting we did together. In the words of philosopher Ludwig Wittgenstein, "If I have exhausted the justifications I have reached bedrock, and my spade is turned. Then I am inclined to say: 'This is simply what I do.'"

This is simply what we do: the phrase now and then sounded in my mind as we passed through the smoky industrial hollows of West Virginia and pressed on into Kentucky. A cool rush of air, as well as a succession of loudly played tapes featuring the music of jazz legends John Coltrane and Ornette Coleman, kept me alert enough to drive for several hours after sunset. Having covered about five hundred miles since noon, we finally stopped at the edge of Crawfordsville, Indiana, a place far short of the middle of our journey. This part of town was exactly like thousands of others near American interstates: a strip of motels and fast food restaurants with overpass architecture at one end and darkness at the other.

The desk clerk had me read a long list of "pet regulations" before I was allowed to sign in. Soon Speck and I were pacing a trash-filled median between the motel parking lot and an on-ramp. His feathering was blown wildly by a strong breeze. Looking up, I noticed that the night sky was filled with stars, and I felt pleasantly cold and isolated. Ranging out together, we had left the mosquitoes and heat and crowded confinement of suburban Virginia well behind us. It was autumn where we were now.

MINNESOTA: RUFFED GROUSE

Suddenly he made off like a bounding hare,
ears flung back, chasing the shadow. . . . The
man's shrieked whistle struck his limp ears.
He turned, bounded back, came nearer,
trotted on twinkling shanks.

—James Joyce, *Ulysses*

At nine o'clock on the second night of our trip, I
pulled the truck to a stop behind Uncle Jim's pickup
on a residential street in St. Paul, Minnesota. My eyes
ached, and I was cold from having driven with both
windows down for the last hour, a measure I had
taken as much to keep myself awake after eight hundred miles as to be washed in the prairie-scented
night air.

Heidi, Jim's sleekly gorgeous German short-haired
pointer, greeted Speck inside the front door, slapping
her paws on the carpet and rearing up gracefully. I
noticed that a small black bag had been attached to
her collar and wondered what it was.

Speck drank a bowl of water in the kitchen, then left with Heidi for romps around the first floor. Jim gestured toward the newspaper's sports section on the table. "According to this guy," he said, "the numbers are way down."

An article reported that opening day of ruffed grouse season had been disappointing; the population cycle seemed to have peaked the year before, and the birds had also been hurt by a wet spring.

As I finished with the newspaper, Jim held up a tiny two-way radio hanging from a lanyard and explained that Heidi's black bag contained the other half of the pair.

"People who climb mountains use these," he said.

"Crazy people," I said.

"Some of them might be, but it doesn't matter. These radios are waterproof and work fine at two miles."

"How much?"

"A lot less than you would think."

"Works like a charm?"

"Except when the bag gets torn off," Jim answered, nodding his head. "We've come close, but I haven't lost one yet."

"You don't have to yell and scream?" I asked. "Or whistle?"

"I say 'Heidi' and she comes back," Jim responded.

"In fact, she comes back whenever the thing makes a sound."

A pair of larger radios was then produced; we would be using them to stay in touch in the impenetrable woods north of Bemidji.

The next morning, I felt the chill air as Speck and I passed through a small vestibule that separated the front door of the house from the living room and moved out into the frost and leaves of the front yard. Jim was busy sliding cased shotguns into his pickup and accepting wishes of good luck from neighbors driving off to work.

Speck led me across the street, then took me, before I knew it, around a soccer field. Given that he was full of nervous energy after two days in the truck, I wondered whether I should crate him—not let him hunt—until Grouse Camp had come to an end. When hunting the same territory in years past, I had felt the Minnesota ruffed grouse woods to be as immense and featureless as a deciduous ocean. Each direction had looked the same until it seemed that a bird dog could go out of sight one second and cease to exist the next. In fact, Speck had once disappeared for a long hour before our paths finally crossed in a marsh littered with fresh deer sign. Wild-eyed and bleeding from the tongue, he appeared at my back, seemingly out of nowhere, finding me before I could find him.

Far greater than my fear of losing Speck, however, was my desire to see him run. I owed him a chance to become a bird dog again after so many months of heat, check cords, and long days in the house. I opted to cut Speck loose in those sprawling woods.

On the road to northern Minnesota, the spruce gradually gave way to aspen and the busy interstate to a maze of frost-heaved highways that Uncle Jim seemed to know as well as he knew the streets of his own neighborhood. Somewhere far from the village of Turtle River, a gravel road brought us to the shores of a loon-infested lake that was colonized around the same weekend each year by a compact nation-state of grouse hunters: brothers, coworkers, former college classmates, friends in bird hunting alone, and guests like me and Speck.

On a tree by an open campsite carpeted in brown pine needles hung a piece of paper that claimed the place for Jim or someone named "Lefty," whomever arrived first. Adjoining campsites had been settled with tents and campers but most of the four-wheel-drives were missing on a sunny mid-September Thursday afternoon.

That night, ten hunting dogs—from puppies to twelve-year-olds, from golden retrievers to Brittanies—would roam the campground howling for attention, retrieving discarded cans of baked beans, wandering off into the woods, tangling chairs in check cords, stealing food from the picnic tables, swimming in the lake, and rolling in the sand. But at the moment just two brawny yellow Labrador retrievers could be seen sniffing around the fire pits and gear-cluttered picnic tables. The Labs belonged to Charlie Olson, a former coworker of Jim's. The dogs were hunting their way through the campsites, rather than through the coverts, because Charlie and his brother, Gary, had taken their limits of five birds apiece in the morning and had finished hunting.

Having ensured that we would eat a huge meal of ruffed grouse fajitas planned for the next night, the Olsons lounged in collapsible chairs by their fire pit, sipping Rolling Rock beer. They said that they had been crawling since sunrise over and through massive deadfalls—tangled, nest-like piles of felled trees that timber companies had knocked down during clear-cutting but had not removed, and around which the forest had grown back. Hunting these deadfalls meant turning their backs on the ease of the open logging trails where the birds would loaf and eat clover in the peak years of the cycle. Was this technique at odds, I wondered, with Speck's gift for flying toward the horizon?

After talking with the Olsons, we found Jim's friend Don, who had arrived a few minutes before. In fifteen minutes we had set up camp and were ready to leave for the grouse coverts nearby. As Jim stepped into the cab of his pickup, he said something about a lonesome pine tree.

"What?" I asked. "Say again?"

He cracked the window and said, "It's hard to explain, but it's a funny-looking tree. You'll see it later"

Don joined Jim in the pickup, and I followed in my truck. On the half-hour drive to the state forests, we headed down and across several empty highways and passed through a network of gravel roads that dissolved into dust clouds.

We parked along a state forest road, unloaded the dogs, and divided the covert three ways. Soon Speck and I stood at the head of a ten-foot-wide ribbon of access that a logging operation had cut to harvest spruce. The surrounding clear-cut had been reclaimed by a hot jungle of aspen, red maple, knee-high grass, and thorn-encrusted vines and bushes. Scattered across this dense landscape were deadfalls from which leafless branches protruded in every direction. I heard a shot from the the trail taken by Don and his diminutive springer spaniel, Molly. This seemed to be a promising sign.

Speck pulled the leash tight, leaning into it and straining to go. What he wanted was plain: to have all restraints—whether check cord or leash—finally dropped. I whoaed him, unsnapped the leash, and began to load my shotgun.

As he waited for me to fish out a second shell, Speck fixed his eyes on the woods ahead, nervously lifting and lowering a back foot. Nothing literally connected us now, yet he seemed determined to stand as calmly as he could manage.

Saying "All right," I touched the top of Speck's head with my hand, and he broke out into a sprint. I shouted "Birds!" to let him know that he was right to put some space between us, not that encouragement was needed. In an instant, he had soared over a deadfall, with offhand grace, like a deer clearing a fence.

During the next few hours, Speck sometimes crisscrossed the logging trail, the way I imagined George Bird Evans's Old Hemlock setters did; or he traced, with unaccountable precision, parallel lines about fifteen yards to the trail's sides. Other times he hunted at a sprint that threatened to take him out of our territory and into parts unknown. Whenever he passed by, I could see that his eyes were blank, oblivious to everything but the immediate world within.

As we hunted, I would catch a suggestion of movement or even a flash of white behind the curtains of green and yellow leaves—Speck's high, feathered tail was proving to be a useful marker.

When he went completely out of sight, I could sometimes hear the tremendous racket he was making as
he crashed through the underbrush.

Unable to believe that he was really out there
unless I could see him, I blew the whistle frequently
so that my eyes could confirm the fact of his existence. The sight of him had a strange effect on me. I
would forget where I was supposed to be going as I
watched him race through the woods with an always-
building velocity that made me ecstatic at least as
often as it made me anxious. Speck seemed to be
possessed by, rather than simply invested with, a
desire to find birds, and it was beautiful to see him
lost within his great and maddening need.

It seemed unlikely that a ruffed grouse—however
much a fool hen—would hold for a point given the
intensity of this attack upon the covert. Nonetheless,
I was concentrating mainly on keeping Speck within
reach. I wanted to be close enough to see how wildly
he was throwing himself at the world.

Soon he led me to a grouse that could not be
killed, at least not by me—a bird that seemed to be an
immortal god. It rose slowly through each of my inept
shotgun blasts as Speck whirled around the leaf-
strewn earth on which it should have fallen. Three
times we caught up to the bird, thanks to Speck's solid
work, only to be left behind. I watched him begin a

new cast and walked forward down the trail. When the silence wore thin, I blew the whistle to turn him, once more, in my direction.

. . .

At Grouse Camp that evening, after a day on which the birds were scarce for most of us—excepting the Olson brothers—a dozen hunters sat on collapsible chairs around a fire. The flames roared up out of a large, rusted metal cylinder that had been sunk into the ground. Split logs were stacked beside the cylinder. Now and then, Lefty (the hunter we had beaten to the campsite) would reach over and drop a log into the fire.

The men stared at the flames intensely, as if trying to identify a pattern, and listened to a story about hitchhiking through the West some years ago. Shadows flickered across their jackets. The speaker, a stout man with a patchy black beard, said in his robust Minnesota accent, "I'm stuck in Rock Springs, Wyoming, without a dime to my name. This truck comes out of nowhere, okay, and pulls to a stop. I'm wearing a pair of overalls I found in a trash can. I have gigantic sideburns—"

Before he could go on, two men shouted an identical curse so sharply that our hearts all but stopped. An adorable golden retriever puppy named Gunner had leaped from the shadows and knocked over their cups, which had been filled with whiskey on crushed ice. Other dogs tried to lap at the puddle of spirits but were shooed away. The whiskey drinkers began profanely busting each other's chops, and, as the hitchhiking story resumed, I let my mind wander across the campground to Speck, who was, much to my relief, safely asleep in the truck, his high spirits sure to be in check until morning.

I found myself thinking about how, when Speck was a pup, he would fight the check cord linked to his harness, rearing up and flailing his front legs as if the rope were a snake that had attached itself to the flesh of his back. In time, though, he had learned to tolerate the shifts being forced upon him, to anticipate the check cord's stubborn halts, and to advance through the field in accord with the ritualized zigzag of bird hunting, going one way for just so long before turning, constantly abandoning one route and taking up another in order to get where we were going.

As much as the check cord was a device to compel and shape movement, it was also there to impose range. It was a physical limit—twenty, fifty, even one hundred feet—that you carried with you and unrolled when needed. One could imagine check cords that stretched for miles: In many places on the public grasslands in South Dakota, nothing would have interfered with such a supercord's continuous paying out, which would have been as smooth as the descent of an anchor rope to the sea floor.

The trick of using a check cord was getting to the point of not needing it. You wanted the physical limit to become an idea that your dog respected, so that the literal thing—the cord itself—was fully replaced by a metaphor of it. You achieved this transformation through repetition. The more familiar the check cord became, the theory went, the more expendable it became, until finally, in its tremendous unspoken thereness, it no longer needed to be present.

Speck fell for this trick during part of one season. I removed the check cord and it remained there between us, as planned, yet his ability to honor the illusion succumbed, in time, to his drive for less structured explorations of range. That, I realized, was when I had picked up the whistle in earnest, and I had rarely put it down since.

Later that night we ate strips of grouse meat and watched the fire. Lefty, evidently communing with the ghost of outdoor humorist Ed Zen, told some amusing stories, more or less real-life episodes in which the joke was always on him. He also said that October was his favorite month by far, because of how cold it was at night, and everyone agreed with him.

At one point, after the already silent woods had

grown silent by an additional degree, I noticed that the hunters across from me were looking out at the beach.

"What is it now?" one of the men asked.

"Big wrestling match," responded another.

Turning, I saw four or five dogs at the edge of the lake. Sand was flying in the moonlight.

"Aren't they tired?" asked the first man.

Now we could hear splashing water and puppyish barks.

"Let's face it," said the second man, sipping his beer. "Dogs are weird."

To us they are, I thought. The dog province that had formed in the midst of Grouse Camp—they had already pieced together a sort of culture with their own rules and hierarchies—did seem downright mysterious from our own remarkably limited point of view.

An hour later, I left the circle of hunters and walked to my truck. I opened the tailgate and there was Speck, curled up in his nest of towels. He barely stirred as I smoothed the fine white hair between his eyes. No one, I told myself, should expect a bird dog to execute, with slave-like precision, a plan drawn up by humans. It was time, then, for the whistle to yield some ground. But the question remained: How much room should I give Speck to improvise?

. . .

On Friday morning we awoke at dawn, picked out a new set of coverts on Jim's map, and made the short drive from the campground to the state forest. After we had parked the vehicles, I watched Don gather Molly from the back of the pickup and walk her to the head of the trail. Whereas Speck and Heidi strained at their leashes in their eagerness to enter the woods, Molly dropped to the ground, rolled over, rubbed her silky fur in the grass, and cutely pawed the air as if asking to play or to be left behind rather than hunt. But why would a crafty hunter and retriever have misgivings about a grouse hunt? There was no way of knowing, but I imagined that she was thinking of the needle-sharp thorns that had bloodied her paws and tongue the day before, and of the rotting meat that had been suspended from mesh bags by bear hunters and scattered on the ground beneath their tree stands. With his hackles up, Speck had growled and barked at the repulsive odor.

The trucks stood next to Lonesome Pine, a fifty-foot-tall spruce that was incongruous not simply because it was the sole conifer and the tallest thing around, but also because it inexplicably had not a single branch except that it blossomed into a triangular miniature Christmas tree a few feet from its top. The day before, while reading Jim's annotated map, I had characterized the name as "melodramatic," but now it seemed perfect.

Don, Jim, and I separated to hunt our assigned patches of cover. The woods were damp and cold. Sunshine glittered in spider webs as Speck and I, hunting mature forest on this morning, passed through an open landscape of moss-covered boulders and tangled gray roots, a gothic wood that seemed too old to support grouse in large numbers. The air around me smelled like wet leaves, like earth. Before long, I could see Speck far ahead, standing motionless near a sizable log that at one time might have been used for drumming.

I thought about taking a picture. Speck looked regal and beautiful, but not intense: he seemed to be demonstrating his wish for more birds rather than indicating one grouse in particular.

Half of the log in front of him was sunk into the leaves; the other half was lit by a slender rectangle of morning sunshine that made the moss-covered bark seem brilliantly green. There was a forester's term, I remembered, for what had befallen a downed tree whose root structure was partially exposed to the air: "windthrow" was the term, and it seemed an apt description of the tree's fate.

As I prepared to take the picture, the radio crackled. I ignored the burst of noise and continued to fumble with the camera. Then I realized that, amid the static, I had heard Don saying something that sounded important. In a moment, his voice had become so clear that I was tempted to check whether he stood beside me.

"Have you guys seen Molly?" he asked, then explained that she had disappeared while chasing a rabbit.

"Let me know if you see her," he said, his voice again garbled and unreal.

Speck and I headed deeper into the woods. A small aircraft flew close to the trees, its engine droning like a giant insect. I heard paws clatter across the leaves, then Jim's low voice, and a lanky German shorthair wearing a small black bag on her collar came loping by me. I was impressed to see Heidi obey Jim's command and change direction.

Having heard no news for half an hour, I decided that Molly had turned up. This was what I always did, at first: assumed a lost bird dog had been heading in the right direction, had been just about to arrive, the whole time.

A few minutes later, though, there were the broken-up words: "I'm really starting to . . . where she is . . ."

I stopped hunting and walked back to the trucks to help with the search. In a few minutes Jim joined me there to wait for Don, who soon appeared. I put Speck in his crate, and Jim did the same with Heidi.

Don said he hoped that Molly was still in the slice of forest they had been hunting, a dozen acres bounded by two trails, the gravel road, and a recent clear-cut that stretched to the horizon. He mentioned that a short check cord was attached to her collar.

"Wherever she is, if she's stuck, we'll have to go to her," he said. "She won't be coming to us."

It was possible that she had traversed the clear-cut instead, putting a vast field of cut tree limbs, stumps, and other slash behind her.

After Don suggested where Jim and I should search, we all fanned out into the cover. Perhaps an hour passed. I stopped again and again to listen, and I thought about the instant photograph I had taken the afternoon before of Jim and Don with two birds. At the last minute, Molly had slipped inside the viewfinder to pose at her master's feet, her nose angled toward the grouse above her head. She appeared to be proud of the birds. Each time I stepped into my truck I saw the image propped against the four-wheel-drive control, and it struck me as a rare good picture.

I could hear whistles everywhere, and, less audibly, shouts of Molly's name. In the middle of the covert, I flushed two fat woodcock that fluttered up and vanished. My gun was open and empty; in any case, woodcock season was still closed, and until we found Molly, I was not hunting for anything but her. The search had finally drawn me into deadfalls that were like island labyrinths within the landscape of regrowing clear-cut. The air was dense, like an invisible fog, inside each sprawling deadfall. When I stood in a piece of sunlight that had managed to penetrate the canopy, the radiant dust made it look as though glittering rain was rising from the ground, as though the woods were dissolving upward. Was Molly sitting out in this light where I could see her, or was she back in the shadows where my eyes and my voice could not reach?

From our disparate positions in the woods, we each followed the sun back to the road, but Molly wasn't waiting by the trucks. Don generously urged Jim and me to hunt while he continued searching. We went through the motions of doing so, but our minds were on the lost dog. Jim commented, "The worst part is being helpless. It's having to wait and hope."

I thought about buying one of the huge tracking antennas used by coon hunters for locating hounds who had strayed miles from their handler. I thought about the writer Rick Bass and his shorthair German Colter, a bird dog of a lifetime who had never come home. I thought about how lost dogs, if given a choice, were always on the move, either heading toward you or away from you.

Molly wasn't simply resting of her own free will, I guessed, because that would have undermined the cause of getting lost—investigating new territory without being constrained in the least or finding the source of some odor percolating on the breeze from miles away.

Jim and I found ourselves hunting through a vaguely lunar terrain of narrow, exposed ridges and huge rock outcroppings covered in mats of gray lichen. Jim said that this was a semifamous spot in Grouse Camp lore. A few years back, Charlie Olson had stood on one of the boulders and shot a grouse flushed by his Labs working the valley far below just after he had paused to think how fitting it would be for exactly that to happen. The season had been one of great abundance, a peak year in which the birds had seemed to sacrifice themselves to Olsons and less lethal mortals alike.

Our path took us past an old house that first had me seeing human faces in the shadows, then imagining that Molly had wandered in through the open front door. While heading back to the trucks, we got turned around, if not lost, but Jim pointed us in the right direction by using the tiny compass pinned to his vest.

Soon the radio crackled, and we stopped walking to better hear the words.

"The eagle has landed," the radio announced emphatically. "Gentlemen: I REPEAT . . . ."

Back at the trucks, Don told us how he had finally found his dog. He had called Molly's name for seemingly the thousandth time, had heard her bark in response, and had begun a sort of conversation with her, one that eventually led him to the spot on which she sat. He said that the check cord had become tangled, just as he had guessed, anchoring the little springer to a slender tree in a shaded spot that was almost exactly in the middle of the acreage he and Molly had been hunting.

"She was probably mad," Don said, "that she couldn't get back here by herself, the way she always does."

"Always?" I asked.

Don nodded confidently, confirming that some dogs would do anything to find their way home.

Molly was in good shape and overjoyed to be reunited with her master, who was just as happy in return but physically worse off, having been battered by the dense woods. I appreciated Don's reasoned approach and hard work during the search and hoped that I would handle things as well if Speck became seriously lost.

I looked back over my shoulder and saw Molly sprawled comfortably and sound asleep on her foam pad in the back of Don's pickup.

. . .

On Saturday, at lunch next to Lonesome Pine, the Olson brothers displayed six grouse. Once again, they advised us to root around in the deadfalls. I followed their advice for the rest of the day, the last for me and Speck at Grouse Camp, and in the thickest cover he pointed several woodcock. Although I did resort to the whistle now and then, we managed to hunt more quietly than usual. Mainly it was the cover, I recognized, rather than some change of heart, some breakthrough for us both, that was keeping him right there with me. But we would take it.

That afternoon, the world was a sometimes soft, sometimes unyielding net in which we had become entangled. As I walked forward, the branches I disturbed would lash my cheeks and the backs of my hands. Stark lines fused just ahead of us to form a solid wall of branches, a horizon so close that the whole of the covert seemed to have shrunk to the small space in which we happened to be moving. This space was bounded above by a low leaf canopy shot through with jagged shapes and coins of sunlight. While the canopy pressed down on our heads, the ground, littered with dead wood, seemed to rise to meet us.

Speck would crawl under the logs that were always finding my shins—the battery case that protruded from his electronic collar broke off pieces of bark when he stood up—or he would fly over them with disciplined leaps before curling his white, speckled body to slither through the young, regrowing aspen thickets. On occasion, I would discover that, rather than go around or duck underneath, I would have to press the saplings down with my weight until I'd bent them over. All of the time, I felt that if Speck and I stopped fighting off the grasping cover we would be caught and held in place.

Near dusk, Speck slid into a stylish point, all four paws grouped around the same center, his head raised high and tilted forward. Two grouse flushed behind a cloak of leaves. There was a brief chase, then Speck located and again pointed one of the short-hopping birds. My final shot of the day was a hopeful attempt that resulted, not in a kill, but in a burst of branches, a harmless bloom of shredded leaves that hung in the air around us, then slowly drifted to the ground.

For Speck and me, Grouse Camp had come to an end.

SOUTH DAKOTA: PRAIRIE GROUSE

Here is the dog, which has always been an
enthusiastic hunter on his own initiative.
Thanks to that, man integrates the dog's
hunting into his own and so raises hunting to
its most complex and perfect form.

—Jose Ortega y Gasset,
Meditations on Hunting

That evening we left Grouse Camp for South
Dakota, which had been our primary destination all
along. It was the place where Speck and I had experienced most often what it was like to become
completely immersed in the chase, where the question of range had sometimes faded into the
background of our hunting together.

After driving two hundred miles across
Minnesota, we arrived close to midnight at the family
cottage on Clear Lake, which was just inside the South
Dakota border. Early the next morning, I called one of
my relatives in the nearby town of Sisseton and

received a polite request to make myself scarce by the first of October so that the pipes did not freeze and the heating bill did not become obscene. I responded that, although I would be leaving frequently on trips to parts west and south of Sisseton, I was hoping to use the cottage as my home base until the last week of October, and that I would gladly cover the heating bill if given the chance. Then I was free to scatter maps and letters on the kitchen table and to finish planning the first of many prairie-grouse hunts.

At my feet, Speck slept with tightly closed eyes, his fully extended body looking sleek without all of the feathering that had streamed from his legs and tail a few days before. He seemed to be at peace, yet wondered whether the short-grass prairie would bring out a deeper wildness that had been held in reserve. And, too, I wondered whether we had a bird coming: the way the Minnesota grouse had eluded us caused me to question the actuality of what we were hunting. If Speck would point and I would shoot what he found, the first bird of the season would prove we weren't chasing ghosts after all.

At 10 A.M. we began our drive to a large tract of public grasslands lying one hundred fifty miles away, in central South Dakota. Although we slowed for numerous combines heading to soybean fields and were stopped regularly at construction projects related to several years of heavy rainfall, we were in the field no more than four hours later. A white afternoon sun flared above us, and soon the grass seemed thicker than it had in past years. Speck chased several meadowlarks and a jackrabbit with stiff white ears and completed a few long casts before his flanks began to heave. We drained my two-quart water pack, sat in the bare shade of a fence and waited for the heat to break. When the clouds shifted somewhere high above, the temperature dropped so much that I could feel the difference on my skin.

In the dissipating heat, we walked a few miles to a pond around which sharptails and prairie chickens sometimes loafed on sunny days. Amber light struck the grass, lending it a reddish tint and bringing slender shadows out from the millions of stalks. Our own shadows were so tall and finely articulated that, as we began hunting, their flickering movements caught the corner of my eye, as if we were walking around with delicate structures affixed to our backs. All the way to the horizon, the glowing land folded itself out into plunging draws and smoothly rounded crests, the hill tops becoming smaller and smaller until they resembled buttons near the vanishing point. The grass looked the same everywhere and was very still, like a glassy sea. It appeared to be dense and substantial enough to hold our weight.

Near the pond, Speck stopped running all at once and pointed, as if, in midstride, he had instantly grown too heavy to move himself another step. Then, in the silence fifty yards out, numerous gray brown shapes—sharptails—began peeling away from the grass so swiftly that they might have passed up through the ground in flight. Together the birds swayed into balanced glides, their wings fixed between beats. When the flock grew small, it looked, against the sky, like a magnified swarm of shotgun pellets as it vanished over a crest.

Quartering at top speed in the cooling air, Speck located many more sharptails and prairie chickens in the next half hour, sprinting from one staunch point to the next. In contrast to this fine performance, I managed to miss two medium-range crossing shots and, worse, to fire below a rising, straight-away sharptail that Speck found at the edge of a dry creekbed.

As the hour grew late, Speck displayed his extraordinary drive more fully, hunting at greater and greater distances from the gun. Rather than being filled up when birds were found, the lack he seemed to feel in his heart was evidently further hollowed out by each new satisfaction. He was locating so many birds, and each one was making him so much more aggressive than he had been just a moment before, that I was forced to jog to gain some ground. I was mindful, however, of the decision I had made at Grouse Camp—namely, to give Speck more freedom as we hunted. I blew the whistle to point him toward the good cover high on the hillsides, but I tried not to hack him purely to close the distance between us.

The sun began to set, streaking a distant bank of clouds with pink and orange. Speck glided through the grass with his nose lifted at an angle to the ground, his tail high. He slowed to a trot and then to a creep, tipping his nose up more and more, before he suddenly froze. Standing still on top of a ridge-like crest, he was silhouetted from head to tail against the sky, his feathers moving in the slight breeze.

As I reached Speck's side after a lengthy walk, a prairie chicken flushed from the grass. I mounted the shotgun and missed with the open barrel, swung past the bird, and fired again. It twirled to the ground and began to rise and fall on its feet. It peered around and flapped its wings in a bereft manner. Speck lowered his head, sprinted toward the bird, and tackled it with his mouth. Although there was a wild, glazed look in his eyes when I commanded him to "Give," he immediately dropped the prairie chicken on my boots and turned away to paw the feathers from his tongue.

The first bird of the season lay in my hands, finally and miraculously, so I took care to look it over.

Where my fingers rested after I had parted the soft, barred down of the breast, the bird's flesh was tacky and hot. The mottled feathers of its fanned tail formed a neat band that suggested a ruffed grouse. Assuming that in the spring the tail would have been lifted and spread impressively in a renowned courtship display, I felt a twinge of guilt at having killed the bird, but it was the fleeting guilt of one who could not help himself. The feet were grandly feathered, as intricately textured as the tiny hands of a baby, somehow reptilian at the same time, and a jaundiced light brown in color. The claws were dark, brief, and sharp.

At dusk, as Speck watched from his crate, I got down on my knees to gut the bird. For a moment, I imagined a cleaned bird as inviolate as those returned by the side-street entrepreneurs operating in South Dakota's extensive bird-cleaning underground—matter-of-fact businessmen I had contacted on past trips after reading their fliers on gas station bulletin boards or getting their numbers from motel desk clerks. One cleaner, I remembered, had returned my bloody, matted, wet, and filthy pheasants in such pristine condition they seemed to have been scrubbed with a pressure hose. The pellets had been picked out and the breast meat glowed with pink health. Moreover, the cleaner—his name was "Wild Bill"—

hard-froze the pheasants and delivered them to the motel room for a modest fee of two dollars each. I had also encountered in the back of a motorcycle shop after business hours, two aged men who, with their bloodied hands and porcine faces, would have fit right into one of the English printmaker William Hogarth's grotesque street scenes; on a pool table, their ledger and a mound of one dollar bills sat next to fifty dead roosters and mallards in a way that suggested a depraved form of gambling. Another night, I had pulled up to a house with freshly painted shutters and a beautifully landscaped lawn only to discover that the garage was a reeking butchery. My experiences in the bird-cleaning underground had caused the placid residential streets of small towns such as Platte and Gettysburg to seem like passageways through a busy hive of slaughter.

At my own improvised cleaning table—the prairie ground—I cut off the bird's wings at the joints and slid one into a plastic bag; the U.S. Forest Service, which administers the public grasslands, required hunters to turn in a wing from each bird killed. I used a pair of shears to cut off the head, which I found that I wanted to pick up and finally did, gently pressing a closed eyelid from which a drop of blood leaked. The crop was stuffed with ragged lengths of bright green alfalfa and purplish grasshoppers. Dropping the shears, I used my fingers to rip out the plastic-like tube that leads from the crop into the breast cavity. I separated the skin and feathers from the flesh, turning the surface of the bird inside out. The meat was almost black, seemingly saturated with blood. Half of the breast was abraded and full of feathers pressed into shot holes; the other half was smooth. I used the shears to cut off one foot but left the other alone, as required by law, so that game wardens could see that I had not taken a pheasant out of season. Then I unfolded a knife, jabbed the point into the thin flesh at the base of the breastbone, releasing a dank, sour odor like that of spoiled milk, and began to pull the intestines through the slit. A sharp tug was needed to free the last reddish gray cord. I scraped the underside of the rib cage with my fingers and flicked the heart, liver, and vivid pink lung tissue into the plastic bag, its white surfaces now streaked with dark blood and encrusted with barred feathers.

While I had cleaned the bird, the sun had fallen below a distant crest. I stood for a moment watching the sky drain of all color, and it was difficult to understand that just ten days earlier Speck and I had been trapped in the suburbs. Here was a space the size of Arlington, Virginia, itself but infinitely more empty, without a paved road or a building or another person in sight.

I drove to a small town nearby where Speck and I would stay for more than a week, until the time came to return to the Clear Lake cottage. At a motel with a huge "Gun Dogs Welcome" sign out front and tin after tin of free dog biscuits in the lobby, I rented a cheap but clean room. Tired out more from the past week's driving—I had covered about two thousand miles since leaving home—than from the hunting we had done, I looked forward to a good night's sleep. Once I had settled in, Speck stopped chewing his claws, jumped on the bed, and curled up with his head resting on my chest.

· · ·

For the next ten days, we hunted the one-hundred-thousand-acre public grasslands in the cool of the morning and evening. My shooting remained suspect—I never once connected with the open barrel—but Speck engineered so many good chances that I was able to take several birds. Because he held his points well, no matter how far away he hunted, I continued to use the whistle less often than usual. Sometimes my worries got the better of me, though, and I would hack Speck in for hours at a time.

On the morning of day eleven, I checked out of the motel and drove to a place I called the Corral, a fenced water tank surrounded by short-grass prairie where we had found large, but spooky, sharptail flocks in years past. Given the moderate temperatures and heavy cloud cover, I felt free to divide the day into four hunts—one for each direction of the compass—with the truck serving as the center of things. On our forays, we would hunt large blocks of grassland, each comprising numerous sections before returning to the truck for water and rest.

In the first section, Speck quickly became birdy. When we had come close to a field of green sunflowers growing on private land, he slid into a solid point. As I moved to his side after a couple of minutes, though, he unexpectedly began his own advance toward the birds. I whispered "Whoa" and he stopped, but after I had taken a few more steps he began to gently creep in, as if conflicted between breaking point and standing still. He seemed to be trying to point and walk at the same time, to race me to the birds in slow motion. "Whoa!" I shouted. This time he stood his ground. A moment later, I flushed a couple of sharptails and scratched down the first to take flight.

As I slid the bird into my vest, I wondered why Speck had been shaky on point when the birds evidently had not been moving. Perhaps it was because I was shooting poorly. Perhaps it was because he had caught a young sharptail a few days earlier or been led astray by meadowlarks. Had I reinforced the tendency by killing this bird? I remembered, too, that he had been similarly lax in handling a single prairie chicken the day before. As in this case, it had been necessary for me to walk a long way to reach Speck's point. Maybe the relocations had something to do with the more aggressive range Speck adopted whenever I gave the whistle a rest, thus, with the distance I had to cover before I could flush the birds. Because I was trying my best not to hack him, he was going on point farther away and having to wait longer for me to flush the birds.

The creeping indicated that Speck was fully trained for a suburban park, where he didn't twitch when whoaed, but not for the prairie. It wasn't his fault, of course; it was mine. He could not have been more skilled at finding a single prairie chicken in the middle of an entire section, but he lacked a better dog trainer to lead him through the delicate choreography of point and flush. His increase in range would necessitate more, or different, instruction in "Whoa" and in steadiness generally.

Between the third and fourth compass-point hunts, while Speck took a fitful, panting nap, I sat on the truck's tailgate with binoculars and watched hawks. A small raptor that had been circling lazily for a long time suddenly dove straight to the ground, flushing three sharptails from their afternoon resting cover. Looking forward to being on home turf, I had been saving this section for last because its distant corner lay within sight of the Corral. I felt childish annoyance at the hawk, but my feelings were balanced by the keenness of my hope that other grouse were loafing in the same cover.

I turned Speck loose. At the end of a roaring cast, he dropped into a point, then began to creep forward. I yelled "Whoa" and began to run down a two-track winding through the spare grass, with the shotgun held high in one hand as my eyes checked the ground for holes. Only in retrospect did the futility of this act, not to mention its stupidity, become clear to me. At that moment, I wanted only to reach a distant spot as quickly as possible. Still, I was far from Speck when he broke point and flushed a large flock of sharptails. He ignored the whistle as he chased them to a distant fenceline. I shocked him for disobeying the "Here" command, and he turned sharply and sprinted back.

I praised Speck for coming in and attached the leash to his collar so that we could both catch our breath. Then I tried to reason with him, as if he could understand what I was saying. Yes, I could shoot better, I admitted. Even so, we would need to share the work or the birds would keep the upper hand.

Speck stared into the distance as I talked to him, but, when I finally fell silent, he looked up at me in a friendly, eager way. He was asking me, I suspected, to undo the leash; I knelt down and gave him a quick hug instead.

I knew that I should tell him something important, or teach him something useful, but I didn't know what it was, exactly. If we didn't have roles worked out, there didn't seem to be a way of doing it at this point. It was too late to go back, but it was, also, too soon to start over. We would just have to get along, I told myself, worry about gradual lessons and patient reinforcement at another time, and hope that we would begin to figure things out together. We were changing the manner in which we hunted, and there was bound to be some confusion along the way. I spoke softly into Speck's ear about the birds I had killed over his points, then turned him loose.

Ten minutes later he located another flock of sharptails and staunchly pointed them, but I blew, a good chance to take the last grouse that flushed. I fired twice and the bird cartwheeled and fell hard. Then, when Speck was just a few feet away, it stood up and flew into the adjoining section, using both wings and tut-tutting. I held an empty shotgun as the bird rose into the sky and disappeared.

It was time to settle in for the night, so we walked back to the truck, in which we would be sleeping to save the cost of a night's lodging. I sat on the tailgate and bird-watched as the sun set, studying the flock of meadowlarks gathered at the Corral and listening to their distinctive cries. It got icily cold, the wind becoming loud and starting to rock the truck gently on its wheels. Speck chewed his claws for a while; I read part of a Thomas McGuane novel, *The Sporting Club*, by flashlight; and we both fell asleep.

That night the temperature dropped well below freezing and I had a bluntly symbolic dream that Speck was swimming through the grass, reaching out large hands for more and more territory.

I heard his conversational grumbling shortly after dawn. With my neck stiff and arms and legs numb with cold, it took me a moment to grasp how much the world had changed since sunset. The scene of Speck's deft handling of the second flock of sharptails had become white; the crest barely visible the evening before had vanished behind sheets of blowing snow. The only thing more strange than winter in September was the herd of bison watching us from the other side of an electric fence a few feet from the truck's windows. The hulking progress of these counterfeit phantoms from the nineteenth century, their ragged coats powdered with snow, dislodged a sharptail that skimmed past the windshield and kept going straight to the north.

Ten minutes later, Speck pointed the bird well out

front and crept in before I could catch up. I missed the long shot, and that was the last I saw of Speck for a time. I walked in the direction he had taken and blew the whistle constantly, thinking how difficult it was going to be to find a white, albeit speckled, dog in this world of wind and snow. I searched without success for forty-five minutes; then, when I had begun to let the worst fears bother me, Speck materialized on the horizon. As he approached me, he was revealed by increments, gradually taking on more of the actual the closer he got. As he passed by, he burst forth into reality—black spots, angular shape, shining eyes—and made a charging cast to the side. I cut this advance short with the whistle, then gave a hand signal to limit his range. And we fell back, instantly, it seemed, into the old patterns of strictly defined control. For several more hours we hunted this way, hearing grouse but not seeing them.

I finally gave up, and drove to the eastbound highway in a hail of slushy gumbo that settled an inch deep on the roof, as if we had just emerged from a tunnel beneath the grass. It was time to go home and lick our self-inflicted wounds until they healed.

• • •

For a few days, we rested at the Clear Lake cottage, leaving only to practice "Whoa" at Waterfowl Production Areas. In the waterlogged Day and

Roberts County cover, Speck would not be moved; I whoaed him at awkward moments and tried to tempt him into disobedience but never got the chance to correct him. The longest check cord I owned swept back and forth, back and forth, over the grass. There was a note of regal condescension for all nondogs, I thought, in the way he would stop sharply before I had finished saying the command.

At the cottage, I took to walking slowly past a table on which sat an academic treatise about the Prague Linguistic Circle, a group of scholars from the 1920s who were known to say remarkable things about sentences and words and even mere letters, but I rarely stopped to open the book. In an attempt to dispel the guilt of the doctoral candidate who is neglecting his studies, I sat for hours on the porch with Speck and began to write about him and listened to the cottonwood leaves rattle and watched them fall into the lake. The gnarled branches became noticeably more bare as the week went on.

During the long evenings, as a succession of old bowling pins burned in the fireplace, Speck expended his prey drive on houseflies and I cleaned my over-and-under so meticulously that I was proud of myself. Then I realized that I had been using the full-choke tube, rather than the improved cylinder, for my first shot and could not have prepared myself better to shoot a turkey or a goose at long range.

In the middle of the week, when the signs of cabin fever had become too obvious to overlook, we headed out one afternoon and after several hours on an empty highway reached a small town in western South Dakota. The next morning I was to drive to the local convenience store, where the owner of a forty-dollars-a-day guide service—a last-minute find—would be waiting for us. He had sounded drunk on the telephone. My question about prairie-grouse numbers had elicited a barely audible and somewhat confusing answer: they were up for the area, but he couldn't say how the area compared with others. I would just have to come and find out. Neither the customer service blandishments of the hunting lodges located in the more densely populated, less arid eastern part of the state, nor their high prices, had spread to this desolate corner of South Dakota.

Even in the dim light cast by a broken neon sign outside the motel where Speck and I would be spending the night, I could see that all the sidewalks were covered in bird droppings and confetti-like paint chips. The first room had no heat; the second had a broken toilet and mice; the third had no light except for a lamp that went out every time I sat on the bed. There were faint streaks of liquid on the walls and dozens of tiny brown stains on the carpet of every room. Speck would sniff them warily and retreat to a corner.

The next morning, I found my contact in a coffee klatch of bleary-eyed farmers.

"Are you from Virginia?" he asked, evidently trying to feign a Southern accent.

We drove to a house in town where the assigned guide was waiting with two golden retrievers, one of whom held a wooden retrieving buck in his mouth, whimpered hysterically, and shook. I cleared the passenger seat, said the goldens looked nice but would have to stay home, and went as invited into the basement. The two men drank coffee, dipped snuff (or "snoose," as they called it), and had a long conversation about killing an antelope. The talk eventually turned to grouse and then to bird dogs, rattlesnakes, and cactus spines. After what seemed like a long time, the guide and I left in the truck.

He was a slightly built, disheveled man with stringy white hair and a black mustache. He wore camouflage clothing and a sweat-stained baseball cap that said "Copenhagen." He slid a cased shotgun and a cooler into the back of the truck. Before we could leave the neighborhood and return to the highway, he let me know, by speaking so frantically that he was often out of breath, that he was a veteran of the Korean War and a retired game warden from another state. He began to tell the story of his life in hap-hazard order: his tumultuous first marriage; his days in the military near Norfolk, Virginia; his exploits in taxidermy; his boyhood in Minot, North Dakota, where he had been born. It was a relief that, against the odds, the man's chatter was fairly interesting.

For instance, as we drove south of town, the guide talked about poachers. In the early 1970s, he said, he had arrested an insurance agent from east of Minneapolis for driving through a state public hunting area in a pickup as he shot at does, bucks, and rabbits with an arsenal of shotguns, rifles, and pistols. The sport had strapped a dead whitetail to the hood of his truck. Whenever he braked, the carcass would slip to the bumper; he would get out to secure it, then fall to his knees and vomit all over his shirt, wave a pistol, and shout drunken nonsense. The dead deer had turned out to be a skinned but not gutted buck with its hooves and antlers sawed off in accord with a logic that remained mysterious despite the sport's efforts to explain it.

"He sat in my truck, and I didn't understand a word he said," the guide commented. "I made a custodial arrest."

On a lengthy hunt of Conservation Reserve Program land, Speck pointed five spooky birds, but I never got close enough to shoot, even though I was using the whistle to manage each step of his progress through the cover. "I could watch him point forever," the guide said. He took to falling back so that Speck and I could imagine we were alone.

In the early afternoon, the guide was mostly silent in the truck, speaking only to instruct me to turn down gravel roads and to cross section lines on rarely used two-tracks through the grass. He dipped his snoose without spitting and carefully gestured to clarify the route. "If you get high-centered," he said as we drove slowly down a boulder-strewn fenceline, "you can always back her on out."

We hunted alfalfa stubble and volunteer sunflower thickets, long shelterbelts and thick sloughs. Pointing out that most of the farms we passed were abandoned, the guide told me that he liked to take photographs of buildings so decrepit another blizzard would knock them over. Speck led us on a wild chase around one such farm, but we never found the bird, which was probably a ringneck tuning up for the season ahead. We had been looking for gray (Hungarian) partridge, which, the guide said, liked to loaf under the old farm equipment, some of it still a bright John Deere green, and to gather around the rusting pickups without tires or windshields and the toppled metal windmills that littered the defunct cow-and-calf operations.

At one o'clock, the guide started to curse and to wonder aloud about where the birds might be. After making numerous unelaborated references to a bear-mauled fur trapper and Native American fire circles, he said, finally, that he intended to show me a little-known piece of cover where sharptails mated each spring and where they were sure to be resting now. Although we walked in the sun for several hours, we failed to discover a sign of life anywhere on the dancing grounds. The country this far west was dry and dusty, and the grass was brown and insubstantial, offering little resistance to the passage of boots. The high ground we hunted was pressed into benches and conical hills studded with cactus, stones, and flowers. The draws were steep and the dry creekbeds were deeply cracked and colorfully stained with mineral deposits. In this hot and arid place, I sweated through my shirt and sunburned my ears. The guide would disappear behind me, then race ahead on his side of the draw, throwing precise hand signals that suggested drill instruction. I wondered what he was up to out there.

Late that afternoon, as we walked out into a rare working farm, the guide fell into a sort of trance as he watched a distant, airborne sharptail growing even smaller against the sky. "I've got you," he said at length, marking it down on a far-off hillside. I watched

Speck charge out and freeze in place close to where a field of glittering grass stubble met a patch of cut corn. While I was making my way over to flush the birds, a half-dozen sharptails walked out of the stubble about fifty yards ahead of him, began to run down the muddy crop rows, then flew off in a tight cluster.

"Crazy son of a guns," said the guide. "Just like a bunch of pheasants."

I called Speck in and kept him at heel while we traversed a section of freshly planted winter wheat. When the hillside was before us, I tucked the whistle inside the front of my vest so that I would not be tempted to use it: I didn't want to further spook birds that were already on edge. I released Speck into the grass and made sure to keep up, narrowly skirting an open well that was hidden in a snowberry thicket, a black cavern large enough to swallow a man and his dog together.

Speck began to walk gingerly through the cover, his lifted snout leading his body into a series of quick turns as he worked the scent drifting down the hillside. On top of the hill, he flash-pointed for a moment before swerving into the heart of the scent cone and pointing with his head turned sideways. Four sharptails flushed at my approach and flew straight. Absorbed in the shooting, I neither felt the recoil nor heard the report; my intention alone seemed to have done the killing. Speck pounced on the bird, picked it up, started to walk toward me, and dropped it halfway. As I headed over to help wipe the feathers from his tongue, the guide said generously, "That's how it's supposed to happen. That's how it's supposed to be done."

. . .

The next morning we left for a few more days of wandering in the public grasslands of central South Dakota, where we had hunted previously. One evening Speck brought in a live grouse with a broken wing: someone's lost cripple. The draws were otherwise empty of birds. The next morning—a Saturday—I noticed a number of sport-utility vehicle—all with dog crates—parked by the fences along the state highway and two pickups near the pond where we had gotten the first sharptail of the season. I viewed the alien vehicles as trespassers and experienced the sick feeling that goes along with discovering that other people have claimed ground you have unreasonably come to see as yours.

On Sunday we returned to the Corral. Stepping out of the truck, I spooked three prairie chickens that glided off and landed by a gate two miles to the south. On the way to the gate, I saw ponds and stands of trees and herds of cattle at such distance that each landmark appeared in miniature. Watching a herd of black Angus that looked, from miles away, like sunflower seeds at my feet, I sensed the vastness of the land working its way inside my mind and beginning to make me think of myself as a giant. Speck seemed tiny, during his casts, so small and light and silent out there that he could glide up the draws as slowly and smoothly as the cloud shadows that sometimes floated over the grass.

In the Minnesota woods, I had learned to interpret a spectrum of noise, from the continual scrape of thorns across my field pants and parka, to Speck's crashing through the underbrush, to the violent commotion of a flushed ruffed grouse. On the grasslands, my eyes had taken over; I would fail to hear the swish of grass against my shins until the report of the shotgun reawakened the sense. At the end of a long day, I would even feel that I was standing not in the place I stood but in the far-off place on which my eyes were fixed. Each subsequent step was so insignificant, considering how far I had to walk to catch up with what my eyes were seeing, that I would seem not to be moving at all. And then I would find myself, without having noticed that time had passed, to be standing on the crest of the hill I had imagined myself to be standing on an hour before, as though I had fallen asleep along the way.

We were almost to the gate when I realized that I had not blown the whistle since we had left the truck, even though it had been clenched between my teeth the whole time. More concerned with finding birds, I had simply forgotten to give a single command—not that I had needed to. Speck was racing over the open land with his usual headlong energy, but when he sensed that he had reached a line he would turn sharply and angle his cast such that it crossed the path that I was eventually to take. In this way, as if obeying the pull of an invisible checkcord or the authority of a whistle that could not be heard, he set about establishing a range that we could live with—a comfortable range.

I would have a chance later, I was sure, to try and figure out why this had happened, but I was just as certain that now was not the time for pondering the change in Speck. Now was the time to find the birds that were out there waiting for us.

I slowed down by the spot where the three prairie chickens that flushed from the Corral had disappeared. They had spread and fanned their wings, hovering in place, then dropped out of sight with a sudden heaviness at the base of the gate, which, I now saw, was a rickety wooden structure that served no obvious purpose other than to mark the hill's crest. It did not point the way across a threshold into a new and different patch of land; it led from one empty, windswept place into another.

Moving across the crest, watching the dense grass for an ink-black marking that stood out high on Speck's tail, I had the feeling that, rather than being where I was, I was remembering something, or dreaming about something, that had happened to us a long time ago. Because it was almost white, the pale grass created the impression of snow; the sky was pale and white, as though these uniform expanses were the walls and ceiling of an enclosure. I hurried down the far hillside, soon seeing what I had been looking for. Speck pointed with great precision, his body a straight line, his head so low he nearly touched the ground.

I walked in a wide circle, then moved uphill to Speck's poised body, and a prairie chicken jumped from the grass, flew toward the sky like a gigantic woodcock, and turned sharply to my left. There was the report of the shotgun, and the bird, a yellow-brown shape, stopped in the air, its momentum gone all at once, and fell. Speck eagerly swept the bird aloft, nearly falling over backward. His snout, with its profuse black and brown ticking, was embedded in the breast feathers. Slowly wagging his tail, he jogged over to me and presented the bird.

Another two hundred yards down the hill, where

the still air teemed with dust, Speck pointed a second prairie chicken. The bird flushed wild but flew directly over my head. I fired and a cloud of gray feathers froze in the air, then began to twirl and move, like a handful of thrown leaves. The bird continued forward through this eruption of feathers and silently vanished in a stand of red grass. During the retrieve, Speck's head and part of his chest were hidden behind the bird's soft, shifting mass of banded tweed.

Speck flopped down in the grass panting, moisture glistening on the black, rubbery skin of his nose, his front paws splayed out in front of him, his back legs tucked under his right side. I slid the dead bird into the game bag and sat down. Speck rolled over onto his back to salt himself with the hay scent of the cover and to present his chest for scratching. His fur, wet from the spray of his drink from the water pack, began to accumulate a million particles of grass.

SOUTH DAKOTA:
RING-NECKED PHEASANTS, PART I

Hunting is a path, a muddy, brushy, dank, and
spoor-ridden path along which a seeker, if his
spirit be right, can truly feel the earth. If he is
fortunate, he travels with a true dog.
—Charles Fergus, *A Rough-Shooting Dog*

We remained on the grasslands for another week.
It was a time that I still remember as one of the finest
stretches of the trip. The weather was sunny but cold
enough that Speck could run all day. We got used to
sleeping in the truck, which became like yet another
home. *The Sporting Club*, the Thomas McGuane
novel I had been reading, proved to be not simply a
good book but a hilarious, finely wrought master-
piece. One clear night under the stars, roughly in the
spirit of McGuane's theme of modern-day primi-
tivism, I gutted, grilled on the spot, and, with Speck's
help, consumed a prairie chicken I had killed that
morning.

Speck and I covered more miles on foot that week

and saw more prairie grouse than we ever had before, and the sense that we were hunting together with a shared purpose, rather than conducting moment-by-moment negotiations, never weakened. What had seemed probable a few weeks earlier—that Speck would get lost or hurt, or that he would simply disappear—now seemed unlikely, if not impossible. For a change, I began finding it hard to imagine the worst, and the fears I had always had of losing Speck came to look increasingly groundless and bizarre.

As the days went by, and as we hunted with an intentness that showed we were hungry for the experience, our world came to feel small and familiar, so self-contained that when I finally turned on the radio one morning I found it difficult to believe the date, even harder to grasp that the pheasant opener, which for many marked the true beginning of the South Dakota hunting season, was just days off. In seventy-two hours, thousands of other visiting bird hunters and additional thousands of locals would be swarming through the public hunting areas and the standing corn on private land. Over opening weekend they would kill much of the season's take, which, by late December, would add up to about one million pheasants.

To give us a chance to rest before this special Saturday, I drove back to the Clear Lake cottage. As

Speck took long naps, stirring chiefly to polish off whole bowls of water at a time, I checked the pheasant brood counts published by the South Dakota Department of Game, Fish, and Parks; consulted maps of hunting lands; read my notes from past seasons; and tried to figure out where the birds would be plentiful and the crowds sparse. The answer, I decided, was two Indian reservations not far from Oacoma, a tourist town on the banks of the Missouri River. It didn't bother me that the reservation season had already opened or that this plan would mean going back where we had just come from—central South Dakota. Studying the highway map at the cottage, I felt that most of the state was close at hand, the towns so near it seemed as easy to point to them as it would be to drive to them. The pheasants were supposed to be abundant in the county we would be hunting, yet the reservations would be overlooked by all but a few locals, or so I guessed.

While loading the truck on Friday morning, one day before the pheasant opener, I discovered that a leak in the left rear tire had become critical over night, creating a collapsing rubber doughnut that was not quite flat. I drove at five miles an hour to the Cottonwood Lake Resort on Highway 10 and for a few moments applied an air hose that didn't seem to

work. The tire was hot, and the rim had forged striations into the rubber. Up the road in the town of
Eden, I filled the tire only to hear the air escape with
a sustained hiss. A middle-aged man in a down parka
with the hood up walked over, told me to follow in
the truck, and led me to a welding business on the
outskirts of town. Inside an open warehouse, several
people were hunched over an old ranch gate, their
blowtorches dropping sparks onto the concrete floor.
A radio was playing a ubiquitous and revolting song of
the moment called "Livin' La Vida Loca." One of the
men took off his goggles and walked out to ask what I
wanted. The tire plug cost five dollars.

I put Townes Van Zandt's landmark country-folk
record, "Live at the Old Quarter," in the tape deck,
and we returned to roads I knew well: Highway 25
winding south through Webster, to Highway 212
West, to Highway 45 South in Miller, to U.S.
Interstate 90 West, which led to the Missouri River
and beyond. And so we toured again the state that, in
its threadbare beauty, I loved more than any other.

Each highway was overrun with combines heading
out to harvest corn, with slow-moving grain and cattle
rigs dropping dirt and pebbles that further pitted the
old truck's windshield, and with large luxury automo-
biles and ancient pickups being driven erratically by
the old. I would do my best to pass these vehicles

when I could, but every few minutes I would slow down to obey the speed limits of Ipswich, Groton, Bowdle, Holmquist, Doland, Raymond, and Clark, of Rockham, Zell, and Ree Heights. The brake lights of the police cars that whipped past never flared, even though, as I would later discover, the truck's speedometer indicated that I was going ten miles an hour more slowly than was true.

Clark smelled strongly of the feedlot, but its gas station attendants were unusually nice people. In a convenience store there the owner's family sat around the lunch counter and held an intense fly hunt. An old woman shouted "Get it! Get it!" while raising her swatter. A lot of ditches and sloughs were on fire near Roscoe, the thick smoke rising to form balloon-like masses. Just down the road, next to a railroad track, I saw a tree in which several roosters were perched; the tableau resembled a vivid image painted on a Japanese fan. Pheasants were always flying across the road, but sometimes the rooster I saw in the ditch turned out to be a thistle or the remains of a blown tire. Seemingly, every bridge had a dead raccoon lying on the shoulder. Black cats hunted in the ditches. When I drove down a straight stretch of road with the steering wheel turned to account for a forty-mile-an-hour crosswind and an eighteen-wheeler passed, creating a momentary hollow of calm, the truck would suddenly fly for the borrow pit and the fences and pastures beyond.

Vivian was, in essence, a car-repair garage and two empty buildings. Ipswich had a motel that had fallen apart and fused with the landscape; the billboard out front continued to advertise twenty-four-dollar single rooms but tall weeds were sprouting from the office's broken window. Signs informed me that I was driving through the hometowns of the *Lawrence Welk Show* accordion player Myron Floren (Roslyn), U.S. Senator Tom Daschle (Aberdeen), television personality Tom Brokaw (Yankton), Governor Bill Janklow (Flandreau), and rodeo star Casey Tibbs (Fort Pierre). Other signs said things like "Home of the 1977 State Class B Girls Cross-Country Runner-Ups" and "Home of the 1952 South Dakota 7-Man Football Champion Meadowlarks." Still others announced pheasant feeds at the Veterans of Foreign Wars hall, advertised a "Gold Community" status symbolic of a town's economic strength, and expressed sentiments such as "Hand in hand we work and grow" and "A great place to live."

I missed the election signs—"Farmers for Hunhoff," "Helvig for Commissioner," "Vote No on 5"—that usually stood in front yards in November, but this was an off year, and I contented myself with evaluating countless statues of gigantic rooster pheasants. The largest was in Huron and the most realistic was in Gregory, where, in addition to rooster statues, businesses had put up signs in support of the Gorillas, then playing in the state high-school football championship at the Dakotadome, an indoor stadium in Vermillion. Some towns had collapsing drive-in movie screens and concrete bunkers that used to be dancehalls or rollerdromes. I passed the Sit 'n' Bull ranch, and along Highway 10 I saw Boot Hill—one hundred consecutive fenceposts decorated with old cowboy boots. The miserable Super 8 motel in Wagner rejected bird dogs.

Corn stalks, hay, and tumbleweeds blew across the road, and it was dizzying the way my eyes were drawn down the stubble rows racing past the window. I discovered that the faster I drove over washboard the less I would feel it in my stomach. Signs saying "Think!" marked the places people had died in car accidents. Sometimes the gravel road would cross paths with a farmer's driveway and the mound created there would send the truck flying, for an instant, into the air.

After several hours on the road we reached Oacoma, and I got in an unexpectedly short check-in line at the locally famous Al's Oasis Inn. Al's was a sprawling tourist attraction/hotel located high above the Missouri River on a strip that featured, among other things, a combination souvenir shop and indoor zoo displaying the slogan "We have wolves!" Looking out through the lobby window, I could see huge plastic statues of horses and bison staring out at the traffic. At the front desk, I asked whether a room would be available the next night as well, but the clerk only laughed and shook her head sympathetically. As I soon discovered, there were signs of the imminent hunter invasion: wastebaskets of rags for gun cleaning in the lobby; signs at each entrance directing me to clean my boots with a hose; an immaculate bird-cleaning shed behind Al's restaurant; boxes of shotgun shells stacked by the checkouts at Al's grocery store.

On the rainy Saturday morning opener, it took just a glance at the world to see that hunters were moving everywhere, their sport-utility vehicles standing near them in long rows, their dogs chasing each other through the bustling parking lots of convenience stores and fast food restaurants. The blaze-orange figures along the strip suggested, as I drove past them at forty miles an hour, a mass of blood cells sliding around under a microscope.

I was feeling confident that I had figured out how to defeat these opening-day crowds until, an hour later, I stepped inside the hunting lodge at one of the Indian reservations. A dozen hunters from Mississippi and Oklahoma were drinking coffee and debating which license to buy, while a uniformed wildlife officer gestured at a wall-mounted aerial survey photograph, pointing out circles of crops interrupted by brushy corners, a house where "a nice lady lives who doesn't want people hunting in her horse pasture," and some prime prairie chicken cover by a busy quarry operation. The room contained many trophy whitetail mounts. For no discernible reason, there was a dead canvasback, its wings awkwardly spread, lying on the carpet by a card table.

While the hunters debated whether to pay extra for access to a carefully managed peninsula of pheasant cover, I got in line, bought the special license—my cash went into an open drawer already stuffed with one-hundred-dollar bills—and drove at high speed down the gravel road bisecting the area, picking my way through a team of graders and dodging the trucks driving to and from the quarry. I parked on a bluff overlooking the gray, roiling Missouri River and for a few minutes watched the rain come down and listened to the wind howl.

At first in this harsh weather, which left us cold and dripping wet, Speck seemed a little bit wild. Then he came unhinged. As I watched him tear down a wide shelterbelt channel between two rows of juniper and put up a flock of pheasants, it was absurdly clear, however demanding the conditions, that our grasslands experiences had wrecked his usual feel for roosters, at least for the moment. The prairie grouse had held well, but the pheasants were running in response to his aggressive searching style, and he seemed to believe that to point would have been to let the birds escape. These were spooky birds that had been hunted every day since the opening of the reservation season two weeks before. Perhaps, too, the abundance of scent and the frequency with which he was seeing large, loud birds had driven him mad. Having caught the scent of a running pheasant, he would accelerate into a dead sprint and, ignoring the whistle and the shock collar, keep going until the bird flew.

When Speck had tired himself some, I managed to get the leash on him and we walked down to the Missouri River. I released him along the wide shore and sat down on a bone-white log at the edge of the foam. I had a foolish notion that these waters would magically restore his sanity, that they would—as the trainer Jim Marti comments—put the little marbles back in the round holes. And I thought about how, halfway through Speck's second year, I began to notice that when we hunted together he seemed to slip away from me, becoming somehow "other," even though we were working on the same task. It was like the oddly familiar strangeness that is created when a very small child, seeing his father asleep but not yet comprehending what it means to be asleep, attempts to speak to him as though he were awake, then notices, with a mystified, unpleasant feeling, that his father isn't there.

Wondering what might be going on inside his mind, I imagined that Speck's interior terrain was becoming wildly peculiar during the hunt, and even when he happened to be hunting close for a time, I sensed that he was beginning to leave me behind for a place in which only he felt at home.

There was no crisis here; it was simply how things were. It was as if his race through the grass had become like the mental journey a human being takes through the charged landscape of a dream. Dreams, too, have wonders and distorted logic, and a desperate protagonist fantastically driven to get one important thing. And they have that one thing, which is not unlike a wild sharptail—a mysterious, hidden thing that signifies not itself so much as pure desire.

During other seasons, I had taken to watching Speck for signs that he had fallen into a dream-state while sprinting down a cattle trail or bursting through a snowberry tangle. I looked for evidence that his eyes were becoming glazed, that his limbs were beginning to relax, and that his movements were growing more effortless still. I had to use the leash to stop him from moving for even an instant, but that had nothing to do, I decided, with the mental journeys he was taking.

Now Speck splashed into the shallows of the Missouri River and bit the waves and lapped them as they fell back. When he was sated with river water, he turned toward shore, stood very still as the waves rose and fell around him, and stared at me, as if confused about what to do next. He was panting even in the cold, and steam was rising from his back. His fur was now so wet that it adhered tightly to his body like a mottled skin. I yelled "All right" and pointed toward the world behind us, and he came to life again, racing across the wet sand, his pawprints deep and raggedly shaped, then diving into a field of tall, dense grass. I scaled the soft, wet, sliding earth of the riverbank and followed him.

Speck began making short casts to the front, chiefly because of the thick cover, but partly because a calm had settled over him. Instead of sprinting after the birds, he glided through the grass as he worked scent, as if savoring it. In this fashion we stalked several running birds; each chase took about ten minutes and played out at the speed of a very fast walk; each consisted of pursuits that led to unproductive, questioning points and culminated in a scorching point and flush. Twice we found hens. Then we chased down a rooster that crossed a road—it left neat lines of tracks in the mud—and doubled back into cover we had just hunted. The grass got thinner and thinner; there seemed to be nowhere for the pheasant to go. When Speck pointed at the cover's edge, I was thinking I would kill this bird. But the rooster let me walk past it, then flushed behind me, cackling and riding off on a gust of wind. I turned around and missed twice after fumbling with the safety. In the process I lost my hat. Soon Speck pointed again, with his eyes wide and his nostrils quivering. A rooster flushed from the steep bank of a riverside bay and headed toward the stagnant water, downwind again, a red rocket with shaking tailfeathers. I missed that bird, too. "Part of being human," novelist John Updike writes, "is being on the verge of disgrace."

The hard rain became a fine mist, and soon we found ourselves walking straight into an oncoming shelterbelt drive involving more than ten people. As I passed one of them—he was a boy of fourteen or so— a hen pheasant flushed behind the junipers to our right and headed toward us. Someone yelled "Bird!" and the boy threw the gun to his shoulder. I ducked and put my hands over Speck's head in anticipation of a shot that was never fired.

"That was a grouse, wasn't it?" asked the same

unseen person, seeming to chide the boy, who had proved to be a discerning wingshooter. "That was a goddamn grouse!"

The improving weather brought out other groups as well, so I tried to think of a place where Speck and I could chase a few more roosters by ourselves. We walked down a long, muddy road and reached a vast expanse of bleached grass growing thickly behind a farm. From previous visits, I knew that there were no shelterbelts or corn in this piece of cover, which made it unappealing for most out-of-state pheasant hunters. I also knew that it was a tough place to hunt unless your dog understood how to pin spooky pheasants, because there was nothing to stop a bird from running endlessly away from you. In the morning, Speck had forgotten what he knew about trapping such birds through stealth or cleverness or sheer intimidation, but it seemed to be coming back to him.

I turned him loose and he began chasing a pheasant through the cover, which was waist-high and grained against us. We snaked our way two hundred yards to the east, then retraced our steps, before heading north into broad sweeps of even taller grass. My boots and field pants were further soaked by the rain-drenched stalks; my legs grew tired from the strain of raising them high. Speck would strike milkweed here and there with his tail, causing the white stars of down to stream, despite the misting rain, like smoke from the pods.

I wondered if we were following a live bird or the ghost of a dead one when Speck pointed hard and ignored a suggestion to move on. I approached from the front to set a trap, flushed the pheasant, and killed it with the open barrel. And so it went throughout the afternoon: we pursued countless running roosters, and now and then we were able to catch one. Responding to its every move, however slight, Speck would follow the bird, and I would follow Speck. It was a representational hall of mirrors: the pheasant inscribed a swerving figure that Speck reproduced at one remove and I at another, yielding two copies of the original.

Because he hunted at just the right distance from me, I had the pleasure of watching Speck up close, of studying the way he turned a sidelong trace of scent into graceful action. I was fascinated by the minute adjustments he made during the chase—in the way he held his head or altered his speed, in the precise direction he took to reach the bird. Scent was a message that was being slowly revealed to him, or an idea that, moment by moment, was becoming wonderfully clear. In turn, these small responses, as I watched them very intently, told me something about the changeable reality in front of us.

In the past, whenever Speck had ranged out toward the vanishing point, my sense of what was actually going on in the cover at each instant had been less sure. Now I felt that, simply by hunting close, Speck was unknowingly bringing me nearer to himself and to the birds, and thereby teaching me things that I could not have understood otherwise. The absorbed and connected feeling that I had sought for three years but rarely experienced was again set-tling in, just as it had during our best days on the grasslands. It was no different from finally getting at the hidden truth of a world that seems strange, and beautiful as well, from the outside.

As Speck charged through the cover in pursuit of another rooster, it felt good to know that the whistle wasn't needed. For a long time I had assumed that by continually managing his search, with the whistle and voice commands, and hand signals, I had been teaching him to hunt within range. But he was demon-strating, once more, that by letting go of my desire to keep him fully in check I could begin to erase the con-stant need for him to be controlled. With a pup, the truth might have been different, but Speck was coming into his own: all I had to do now, it seemed, was trust him.

Late that afternoon, as we headed back to the

truck, I decided that we had rarely passed a more blissful few hours in the uplands. Partly that was because of how miserably the day had begun, and not just as a result of the lashing rain; Speck's lunatic morning had served to make the afternoon that much sweeter. I was pleased with the way he had pinned running pheasants in open space. He had performed that feat before but had never shown such patience, never been so skillful in reading scent, never given me a better chance to keep up or so much happiness in watching him work. I thought about the large groups of hunters who, all that opening day, had been driving the shelterbelts and walking the corn across South Dakota. I was fortunate, I thought, to have been alone with Speck in the grass, following the wanderings of roosters through him. I was glad to have been chasing birds that were already there, rather than marching straight to the end of the shelterbelt in vague hopes that a few would appear.

I was still thinking about the day's mass gathering of hunters when Speck suddenly froze perpendicular to the path that he had been following and did not move. It was the most literal act of pointing I had ever seen. My next step jumped the day's last rooster, which I killed with the first shot. This bird, too, had flushed from behind my back, but by this time I was practiced in the confused whirling around involved in waving shotgun barrels in the right direction.

Speck found the rooster, picked it up, and dropped it, demonstrating once more that he would retrieve only when he wished to. In an admittedly futile attempt to see the matter from his side, I guessed that a retrieve was literally not necessary, although obviously useful, whenever the bird had been killed already. Clearly, it remained essential in the case of a cripple.

Before leaving for Oacoma, Speck and I sat on a bluff high above the river. We looked out at the Missouri Breaks and the gray waves and got cold in the wind. Both of us, it seemed, were happy to be in that place, satisfied just to sit there and not move. Having killed three roosters after a great effort, we were savoring for a moment what it was like not to be longing for something we didn't have.

Al's parking lot was full that night. Groups of men held loud conversations by their recreational vehicles in the park behind the motel and clogged the board-walk to the restaurant. They filed down the motel hallways with dogs who barked and shook their collar tags. Speck would awaken at the sounds but, rather than growling and sprinting to the door, as he would have done at home, he merely lifted his ears alertly before going back to wagging his tail and yelping during dreams.

On television, Steve Hemmingsen, the stalwart KELO-Land anchorman, delivered an opening-day report that emphasized the economic windfall and included a brief interview with an out-of-state hunter dropping several hundred dollars at a convenience store in Aberdeen, a city to the northeast. The man, a stand-in for all of us out-of-state hunters, who were in the process of introducing roughly $90 million into the South Dakota economy, said, "It's a lot of money, but it's worth it."

Another channel showed footage of a game-farm hunt, the camera fixating on each somersaulting stone-dead rooster. A state wildlife biologist was interviewed; he named counties with improved brood counts and estimated an insignificant 10-percent drop statewide. All of the neatly coiffed Scandinavian-American weathermen said with unwarranted conviction that the absence of previously forecast snow had meant ideal conditions for pheasant hunting.

At midnight I cleaned the three roosters in a shed that the inn had provided for that purpose. The kitchen smoke drifting over from Al's restaurant, which specialized in buffalo burgers, mingled pleasantly with the mild reek of the innards.

The next morning, on a highway streaming in both directions with hunter traffic, we headed to the second Indian reservation I had planned for us to hunt. Once inside the reservation boundary, I drove around for an hour in search of the tribal game-and-fish office, which, the map said, was located just behind a casino. My wanderings took me down the narrow, broken-up streets of a housing project where groups of young men wearing hip-hop fashions sat on front steps and small children rode their bikes in the gutter. Each stop sign had a gold X on it, and the vacant lots were littered with billowing plastic bags. Below a highway intersection, a four-year-old boy played with the garbage that had collected at the mouth of a culvert, spinning around with a half-empty soda bottle and spraying the liquid into the breeze.

I learned at a grocery store that the game-and-fish office was a nondescript house nowhere near a casino and was closed, but that I could buy a license at the store. While the clerk was filling out the forms, a burly blonde-haired hunter, outfitted in camouflage, walked in and demanded to use the telephone behind the counter. He was politely refused. When he had left, the people in the store wittily made fun of him and looked at me.

I turned Speck loose at a tribal Game Production Area on the shores of Lake Sharpe. He ran five yards and pointed while standing on a sheet of plastic that had been laid down to keep a row of small shrubs free of weeds. We chased the bird into a neat square of grass, the ground rutted from the tractor that had prepared the soil, and Speck pointed a second time. Glimpsing the rooster running fifty yards ahead, I told Speck to move on, then tried to sprint across the uneven terrain. I approached Speck's third, most intense point, flushed the rooster, and killed it with the open barrel.

Although I appreciated Speck's efforts, the bird had been too easy for us and I had to wonder whether it was as artificial as the cover. I inspected the pheasant for signs of a life lived in cages.

The shelterbelts proved to be full of McDonald's french-fry containers and crushed Budweiser cans that vacationers had left behind. There was a large pile of cigarette butts on top of a bulldozed berm within sight of those concrete, recreation area outhouses with aluminum vents on the sides and a metal chimney. Much of the grass in the Game Production Area had been trampled or burned with tourist campfires. For hours we slowly hunted our way through the treacherous ploughed ground of numerous game-farm-like foodplots, but we found little aside from a rotting pheasant coated with sluggish flies. The stench of the pheasant carried far; even though the air was cold, it seemed to surround us.

We left to search for better cover elsewhere on

the reservation, and that was when I drove the truck over a rattlesnake, the first we had seen. I felt both guilty for killing it and intensely hostile at its power to make me afraid. I found myself thinking that this rattlesnake had cast a shadow over a day that had been dark to begin with. It was sad, obviously, to see how hard life was for those who called the reservation home. In the earth's wealthiest nation, this life was as hard as it could be. It made me sick and angry to recognize what we in America were doing, and would always do, it seemed, to the proudest warriors the world had ever known. About my own life, I had nothing to complain of, I knew. But there was something mindless and self-indulgent in my bad mood, and I couldn't help looking at what awaited me back home. Nor could I prevent myself from feeling depressed about it.

I was thirty years old. I had no job prospects and would soon have no money. It occurred to me that I was choosing to hang around with my bird dog rather than devote the time and effort needed to transform myself into a respectable American citizen. I soon realized, however, that I didn't care as much as I should have, and this failure on my part made me wonder if it might be possible to piece together some sort of sustainable existence with a half-wild bird dog at the center of it rather than all the other things I could think of. As long as I could keep Speck close, I could at least take pleasure in watching him run—he was a beautiful sight—and maybe that would be enough. I had the feeling that, when he blistered his way through the grass, he was teaching me something, that his seeking helped me to think about my own. It might have been something about not giving up the search until you had found what you were looking for. Not that I knew what that was, exactly; there was just more walking, more hunting, stretched out before me, and more of learning to tell the difference between self-pity and an authentic reason to mourn. And so we kept going.

From the truck, I saw a second dead rooster, this one wedged between a mailbox and a telephone pole such that its beak pointed at northbound cars, evidently for comic effect. We walked past several hunting parties, and I saw a pointer and a setter playing with songbirds on one side of a hill while the hunters on the other drove the grass in the opposite direction. The two factions seemed at odds.

As we pulled into a new Game Production Area and parked on the shoulder of a busy highway, I thought I recognized the land from pictures that had run with an article about the celebrated prairie-grouse hunt held on the reservation each September. Twenty yards in I had come to feel that I wasn't walking so much as wading. This was the most uncertain ground of all; it not only had the character of ploughed soil that has frozen, with its narrow valleys and rock-solid clumps, but it also seemed to bear the shallow impressions left behind by cattle. I fell as I tried to negotiate the rough hillside leading us to the banks of a slow-moving creek where the cover was thick and beautiful, but I could see the fall coming and barely felt the ground.

Many uneventful hours later, I was on my hands and knees again in an effort to get myself underneath a barbed-wire fence and to my truck while keeping Speck leashed and safe from the heavy, high-speed traffic. Before I could stand up, a battered dog trotted toward us while wagging its lowered tail; it had been sleeping under the truck. Speck growled so softly he seemed willing to befriend the stray—a rangy pointer/Labrador retriever mix, perhaps, with a bright purple bruise across his yellow white muzzle, a scar on his chest, and a therapeutic plastic walking boot on one foot—but I decided to pick Speck up, carry him to the back of the truck, and place him in his crate. To make up for the slight, if not for the sad dog's miserable luck, I gave the stray a few Milk-Bones before we left for Oacoma.

The last thing I remember seeing of this reservation world was the guide service positioned directly across the road from the second Game Production Area we visited. Where were the birds? Except for one uncanny rooster, had they been killed before we had shown up in hopes of doing some killing of our own? The local news was right: pressure was general across central South Dakota.

SOUTH DAKOTA:
RING-NECKED PHEASANTS, PART II

Ain't he a bird? Say, ain't he a bird? Look at
his flag; it's perfect; and see how he carries
his tail on a line with his back. . . .
—Frank Norris, *McTeague*

After leaving Oacoma, we took some time getting back to the Clear Lake cottage. Over several days, we hunted our way gradually eastward and stayed at a different motel or campground each night. We found a few roosters, but there seemed to be just as many other hunters at my favorite areas as there were birds. Competition for space on the public lands had rarely been more fierce. At the cottage I found myself feeling tired of the crowds and of driving, too. Mindful that we had just two weeks of our trip left, I decided that we should stay close to home for the next several days. There was a problem, though, with this plan.

Sisseton, and much of the rest of northeastern South Dakota, had experienced five or six severe bliz-

zards in the winter of 1996. In a March storm at the
end of that brutal winter, I remembered, my cousin
and her husband and daughter had been hard pressed
to keep their calves alive. One newborn they had
tried unsuccessfully to warm in the bathtub of their
home. When Uncle Jim drove down Highway 10
through Sisseton the evening before that storm, he
saw a flock of roosters milling at the edge of a shelterbelt by the Little Minnesota River. It was bitter cold,
the birds were not themselves, and he guessed that
they weren't going to make it to spring. Soon the state
confirmed that this was so: the pheasants had frozen
to death by the thousands.

For three years there had been few signs of a
rebirth. The 1999 brood counts remained astound-
ingly low—an article published in a regional
newspaper had compared hunting for pheasants in
counties such as Roberts, Day, and Marshall to
looking for water in the desert. On the other hand, the
difficulty of finding birds would be a blessing; we
would have to ourselves the many large public
hunting areas located in this weather-blighted territory. After dismissing second thoughts, that was how
I proposed to spend the second-to-last week of our
trip: on a quixotic quest for roosters in northeastern
South Dakota, driving no more than ninety minutes
from the Clear Lake cottage to hunt for needles in

haystacks. I would still get to watch Speck run, and if we found just a few birds I wouldn't try to shoot one.

On the first day of this local expedition, I headed as far west as my ninety-minute rule allowed. I drove the last several miles with my *Sportsman's Atlas*, a book of maps showing all of South Dakota's public hunting areas, propped against the bottom of the steering wheel. Every so often I glanced down at the map to count the sections until a crucial turn, then looked up to make sure that the printed grid and the scene outside matched. Whenever I glanced to the side, the corner of my eye caught marginalia on the atlas pages giving dates, descriptions of Speck's exploits, and numbers of birds seen, flushed, and killed. Memories of other days in South Dakota became tangled up with what the map and the world it represented showed.

At the first hunting area, a tract of more than six hundred acres, I found pickups staking claims to each piece of cover where grass and wild sunflowers grew to shoulder height or weedy cattail sloughs alternated with dense shelterbelts. We had a choice: get right back in the truck and find another place to hunt or try eighty acres of grass stubble. Only this scarred plain, which had been mowed to within an inch of its life, had not been claimed by other hunters, and for obvious reasons. Still, I decided that Speck would enjoy racing across the open terrain. It was a cold, sunny day. The wind was gusting from the west as I turned him loose.

Rather than quartering, Speck sprinted on a perpendicular to the wind. When he had found the middle of the long field, he suddenly turned to the west and pointed with his right paw lifted, his tail high extended at a forty-five-degree angle with the ground in a way that reminded me of Remington, who had, I remembered, hunted here with me and John in the early 1990s. I walked in and killed a fast-flying rooster. Despite my vow to show restraint, I had immediately fired the shotgun out of thoughtless desire.

After collecting the bird, I released Speck and he returned to his linear sprint. Near the end of the field he again turned upwind and pointed. The first of two roosters to flush was a young-of-the-year fool that flew right at me. Its iridescent breast sparked coppery orange and flamed with sunshine; the bird seemed as large as a goose. I shot above it. My faith in the well-documented scarcity of pheasants had made me more inept than usual.

When Speck reached the end of his unswerving path at a fenceline, he pointed with his entire body facing forward, then slowly turned his head to the west. I walked fifty yards upwind, flushed three roosters together, and shot the one in the middle. Speck found the bird, picked it up, and waited for me to take it from his mouth.

Hoping merely to see a single rooster, we had instead come upon what seemed to be the most densely populated ground in South Dakota, a bare place that Speck had sliced up with long casts ending in solid points. There were unseen currents out there that only he could understand—he had read the wind perfectly—but I was grateful that I was near enough to follow along, and that I could do so in a silence unbroken by the whistle. This silence was appropriate, I felt, to a sight I couldn't help but find intriguing. No matter how many times I see it happen, I will never think it mundane when Speck races in a straight line along the edge of a breeze, stops with a jarring suddenness, and points directly upwind a long way from where the birds are waiting and listening.

Everywhere we went that day, we found other hunters and at least a few spooky pheasants, demonstrating that we had traveled too far west for the hunt to resemble the hopeless quest of Don Quixote. In late afternoon, we returned to the spot where we had begun the day and hunted dense cover around the stubble field. After a long chase, Speck pointed in front of a fence. Hearing the bird in the grass and feeling sure that it was a rooster, I walked in while raising the gun for a simple going-away shot. The bird flushed and seemed to be doing as I had guessed until it collided with the barbed wire, narrowly avoided landing on Speck's back, and fell into the grass. There was a commotion as the fence shuddered, and Speck thrashed around. The pheasant gathered itself, then ducked underneath the bottom strand and, unseen by Speck, ran across the stubble, its head tucked into its chest, its legs not perceptibly moving. When it finally flushed a hundred yards away, I heard a loud cackle. The tactic was unconventional but effective: I never had a chance to shoot.

That night, back at the Clear Lake cottage, I cleaned the roosters in the dark front yard, a high wind coming in off the lake, sweeping up the loose feathers, and blowing them into my face. It was somewhat tempting to think that it was easy to kill a pheasant. But as I remembered our hours of fruitless labor at several hunting areas and Speck's achievement in the stubble, I decided that it was always a struggle to take even one public land rooster.

Lying awake in bed that night, I realized that I had been wearing field pants, polypropylene shirts, Gore-Tex socks, and the like (what the inimitable writer Datus Proper called "armor") every day for more than a month. It was awkward now to walk on cement rather than earth—this was true, and it made me wonder—and to wear shoes rather than boots. Speck and I had each lost seven or eight pounds, as much from the hours of walking as from our ascetic diets and the strain of being on the road. His ribs showed, his hindquarters rippled with muscle, the ticking on his skin could be seen, and his feathering had completely disappeared.

I turned on the light and interrupted Speck's claw-chewing ritual to inspect the tiny, scabbed wounds on his legs and put pressure on them, trying to tell whether they were bothersome. He gave no sign that this was the case. They would harden each night and each day the cover would irritate and sometimes make them bleed, just as the tip of his tail would bleed after he had raced through a cocklebur patch. Underneath the fur of his chest I could feel scabbed striations left by thorns and perhaps barbed wire. These wounds were not serious either, nor were the pink abrasions of the whiskered skin at the end of his snout. The worst problem had been a piece of husk that had lodged under one of Speck's eyelids for an hour; on its own, it had risen into the open, where I could gently remove it.

After close to five weeks of hunting, I would fail to notice that I was carrying the shotgun because my arms no longer sensed its weight, and Speck would negotiate barbed-wire fences with such unconscious precision that he could approach at a run and make a darting leap between two strands. Once he had simply jumped a high fence that had surprised him in the middle of a sprint, grazing the uppermost strand with a claw before sailing over into the next pasture.

As I turned off the light and Speck returned to his ritual, I felt he shared my sense that bird hunting was beginning to become a way of life. What he didn't know was that we would be living this way for longer than originally planned. I tried, but I could think of no good reason to head home any time soon. We would just keep going, I decided, until our money or our luck ran out.

The next day we hunted somewhat closer to Sisseton, finding about thirty hens and ten roosters, one of which I crippled at close range and lost, tainting things, making me feel the need to confess and be absolved of my wingshooting sins. Other hunters were always there before us. The closer we got to the Clear Lake cottage on subsequent hunts, the fewer birds and the fewer hunters we saw, until finally there were none of either. I rested the shotgun on my shoulder and watched Speck run as we passed through shelterbelts and grass plantings that had been elaborately prepared for birds that did not exist.

One Wednesday we visited a public hunting area up north at which Remington's ashes had been scattered because, on a celebrated October day in 1986, John had taken three roosters there over Rem's points. The birds had been plentiful that year, but ever since, even before the deadly blizzards of 1996, their numbers had dwindled with a steadiness that was as mysterious as it was dispiriting. Finding nothing alive at the hunting area to the north—and at many others—I began to lose the visceral alertness that differentiates hunting from walking, my diminishing concentration slowly moving me outside the natural sphere of which I had recently felt so much a part.

On the drive back to the cottage I thought that a "No Hunting—School Zone" sign was, in a strange way, forlorn. It appeared to be a sad relic of a time of abundance, not simply of birds but of tourist traffic, money, main street prosperity, and young families as well. In some towns, just a few houses had signs of life: Halloween-orange leafbags propped by mailboxes, wagon wheels embedded in lawns for garden borders, and posters supporting the high-school football team. Whole residential blocks were deserted; some of the business districts, too, consisted of little other than shuttered post offices and grain elevators. The few going concerns were low-overhead enterprises such as craft shops and hair salons or tiny bars with hand-lettered signs. The handsome brick buildings beside them, with bay windows and railing-lined steps leading to the sidewalk, were now empty but still carried the names of the law offices and furniture companies they had once housed. With the world near the North Dakota line so dead, I guessed that only wild pheasants had the power to bring it back to life.

The next day we were again hunting in this northern landscape when Speck pointed by a cattail slough. I walked over and flushed a late-hatch rooster whose colors were just beginning to darken and change. Glimpsing its stubby tailfeathers and orange yellow breast, I did not attempt to shoot the juvenile bird, which I chose to interpret as a sign of better times to come. It soared above the cattails and disappeared.

. . .

"Are you getting your birds?"

A red-faced giant stood before me. Garbed in a pressed business-casual outfit, as if anticipating a steak dinner in town, he had emerged unexpectedly from the basement of a private home in which my brother, John, my uncle Jim, and I also were staying. It was a Friday early in November by this time, some two weeks after the season opener, but the motels in this pheasant boomtown were still booked up. The giant, who turned out to be from Alaska, controlled all of downstairs; we had a large room at ground level.

For the past ten days, John (who had driven from Virginia), Speck, and I had been wandering from the hunting areas around Clear Lake, to the public grasslands at the center of the state, to the territory around Yankton, near the Nebraska border. At times we had notions of tracking down bobwhite quail, which were as prized in the South Dakota uplands as permit (a sought-after game fish) were on the flats of Belize. In the end, though, we spent most of our time simply doing what we liked most: chasing smart roosters through immense tracts of bleached grass for five or more hours at a stretch.

After our days of wandering, John and I did some visiting in Sisseton, catching up with our aunt and cousins and their families. From Sisseton we traveled south and west once more, this time to meet Jim and our friend Clarence, a kind, humorous, and amazingly youthful man who had eventually become the principal of Sisseton High School from which Jim and our mother had graduated in 1953.

Now, as Speck looked on with evident suspicion, the giant was asking me the question everyone asked in South Dakota. It meant, Are you "filling out," taking your limit of three roosters every day? Are you killing the maximum number allowed by law every time you go hunting? Fellow hunters asked me the

question, but so did townspeople at the gas
station/convenience store and motel clerks who
noticed my field pants, and so did my Sisseton relatives and people back home, and so did the outdoor
magazines and books, in their own implicit way.

"Did I get my birds?" I said. "Well, let's see—"

"We got forty-four on the farm last week," he
interjected. "We worked hard, but we got our birds."

Why forty-four? I wanted to ask. That was one
rooster short for three people hunting five days, so
which unfortunate had bought the drinks? Before I
could get a word in, however, the giant withdrew
from the upper level, whispering as he descended
that the best hunting land near Presho had been
leased to the Las Vegas Mafia. A moment later, John
and Jim returned from running an errand, and we
drove off to find Clarence at his farm south of town.

Unlike those on the public areas, this private-land
hunt held the clear promise of limits, offering an
experience familiar to most visiting hunters—hunters
who paid dear prices for each dead pheasant—but
somewhat foreign to me and Speck. Based on the
many brochures I had collected from chambers of
commerce throughout South Dakota, I knew that the
average price for a full day of hunting at a pheasant
ranch hovered around three hundred dollars, with
most outfits presenting long lists of costs not covered

in the daily fee. Landowners who had not yet decided to convert their farms into hunting lodges for the season nonetheless commanded upwards of one hundred and fifty dollars a day for access.

Not long before, a stranger could have asked permission and hunted for free; those days were gone as a result both of the economic hardship of the family farmer and of a bull-market prosperity that allowed tens of thousands of people to see nothing wrong in spending a small fortune to take a guaranteed limit of five roosters—three wild, two planted. The community spirit that had once obligated landowners to allow out-of-state hunters free access—on the principle that this largesse would attract money to main street and thus benefit the town and the county alike—had given way, justifiably, in my view, to the fleecing of well-off strangers.

A rancher I know expressed satisfaction with this Robin Hoodesque redistribution of wealth from metropolitan centers of other states to rural communities of South Dakota. His only serious concern was that out-of-towners would pay ridiculous amounts to purchase hunting land, thus driving up property tax rates so sharply as to put family farmers out of business and opening the way for the passage, at bargain prices, of South Dakota land into the hands of the same outsiders who patronized the pheasant lodges.

Montanans, I knew, had grown wary of, if not hostile toward, land-shopping multimillionaires for just this reason: concern that the only ranches left would be hobby spreads supervised by gentlemen ranchers garbed in immaculate new Stetsons and Australian-style duster coats.

Although I coveted the wonderfully birdy grasslands and shelterbelts so richly displayed on private land, and sometimes got tired of hunting the same public lands year after year, I found that I admired the family farmer for selling access at a high price. The cash that even a small-time hunting lodge proprietor could make between mid-October and mid-November often represented a good year of agricultural profits. It seemed logical to assume that many of these farms would not exist as family operations if they did not metamorphose annually into hunting lodges. Just as the family farm culture was sustained by hunting dollars, so, too, were pheasant habitat and populations. Some of the proprietors devoted themselves to the propagation of cover that would help the birds survive even the harshest blizzard. It was something of a shame, but an economic reward was much more effective than a conservationist appeal in ensuring that the land was managed to produce booming pheasant populations as well as maximum crop yields.

We hoped to find both at Clarence's farm, where, I reminded myself, Speck would have more chances to retrieve in just a few days than he had gotten on our trip thus far. I also expected to enjoy an immersion in strategy. The fragmented character of the cover, when combined with the wily nature of these much-hunted roosters, necessitated a good plan (or "scheme," as outdoor writer Steve Grooms, an authority on pheasants, has it) if you wanted to get your birds and avoid humiliation at the same time. As we took the highway south, passing the Sunshine Bible Academy and the turn for a Hutterite colony, I considered that, with Speck and Uncle Jim's Heidi on our side, the pheasants might not know what hit them.

We soon found Clarence, who had been inspecting a soybean field, and stood with him and talked strategy beside an old John Deere combine and a grain truck with rows of tiny oval windows in the sides that enabled you to see at a glance the payload level. It wasn't yet 2 P.M., but the sky was so evenly dimmed by clouds and a misting rain that it was impossible to figure out the position of the sun. Looking over the washed-out landscape, we noticed a large group of hunters, also with access to the farm, driving a distant cornfield, their blaze-orange caps bobbing in unison.

That afternoon we left the corn to the other group and hunted patches of grass that grew on ground too wet for the plow. From the start, I noticed that Speck limited his range in accord with these confined spaces. He stalked the birds just as we stalked them, making a great effort not to move too suddenly or to make any sound as we passed through the cover. This delicate searching style seemed to carry over into the gentleness of his points, which told us that there were at least a few pheasants in even the smallest patch of grass.

For me, that first afternoon, the birds flew out of range, and I did not fire my shotgun. However, John and Jim, both excellent shots, easily killed three pheasants of the day at the farm, and Clarence, too, acquitted himself well. Some of the birds Speck pointed, then Heidi tracked down and retrieved them in spectacular fashion.

Later, the giant from Alaska was waiting, eagerly.

"Are you getting your birds?" he asked.

"I got skunked," I replied.

. . .

By 6:30 on Saturday morning we had donned our field pants and coats and were ready to go hunting. That left us with more than three hours to kill before the legal shooting hour of 10 A.M. We used the time to eat breakfast and to stake our claim to the so-called

Dugout, which was a depression in the landscape that, in our years of hunting at Clarence's farm, had come to seem magical and strange. It was just a stock pond in the middle of a cornfield, with steep berms on two sides and tall grass growing all around it, but the water, food, and shelter attracted huge pheasant flocks, which roosted for the night in the grass. Those spooky flocks required intricate planning that sometimes found us huddled together in an icy cornrow on the hill above the Dugout, Speck and Heidi whimpering with impatience, Jim using a sharp stick to draw in the frozen mud our paths of approach.

We drove to the farm and worked out a plan for the Dugout while standing in a cut soybean field nearby. As always, we decided to surround the whole thing, allegedly ensuring that one of us would have a shot whichever way the birds flew. Clarence brought to this strategy session the useful experience of having instructed tailgunners during the Second World War in the art of reckoning angles of fire. We were unconcerned about the fact that the Potter County airspace was too vast to be covered by the shotguns of four hunters. The birds exploited this weakness every time, but their history of success only heightened our frenzied hopes that, on this Saturday, we would finally stumble upon the perfect style of assaulting the Dugout.

At about 10 A.M., Speck and I stalked toward our assigned corner, with Speck pausing before he took each slow step, his whole body quivering. A hen flushed noisily from the corn and flew right over us, so low that it seemed we could have snatched it from the air. Although he turned his head and eventually his whole body to watch the pheasant, Speck managed to keep still when I whispered "Whoa."

A moment later, he pointed at the edge of the Dugout. I walked into the tall grass, and, from their respective posts, John, Jim, and Clarence did the same. A few seconds passed. The world was calm. Then, before our eyes, a sepia-toned photograph from an old hunting magazine, an image of impossible abundance, came noisily and chaotically to life. Wave after wave of pheasants lifted from the grass, beating their wings frantically or gliding with the wind, and filled the sky like blackbirds. An instant before, being silent had been so important to us that our rustling of the husked corn had seemed dangerously loud. Now I was firing the over-and-under, and there were reports to my right, where John was positioned. On the other side of the Dugout, Jim shot twice and two birds fell. I could hear Clarence firing his gun, too, and then the brief damp sound of pellets spattering the corn on the hillside behind me.

When we had satisfied ourselves that no birds

remained in that corner of the farm, Jim released Heidi and she began retrieving the roosters that had been killed as well as crippled. Her example helped Speck, who pointed dead before diving into the cover, grasping the bird by the neck, and presenting it to me. This retrieve foreshadowed something better.

On Saturday afternoon we traveled a few miles from the working farm to the Gunderson Land, which was several acres of pasture with a brushy creek winding through the middle. Here Clarence killed a bird that landed on the other side of a six-strand barbed-wire fence. I called Speck in and told him to "Fetch." He forced his way between two tight strands, sprinted to the bird, picked it up, and ran back to the fence. Then he set the bird down gently in the grass and stood and looked at me. The complexity of the task had confused him, but once John joined me in hollering "Fetch," Speck reclaimed the pheasant, climbed back through the fence with it, and dropped it in my hand, completing the finest retrieve of his life. Such a feat would have been business as usual for Heidi, to whom a retrieving dummy was a thing of fascination; for Speck, however, with his distaste for picking up dead birds when he could be chasing live ones, it was a breakthrough and a cause for celebration.

All that day I had been confirming that, somewhere along the way during our trip, Speck had left his youth behind. I no longer had reason to wonder whether he grasped that hunting involved more than finding birds on his own. Without having to be hacked in, he continued to hunt close, putting forth his usual effort but in a smaller space, racing from side-to-side just as swiftly as he used to run for the horizon but working the cover more thoroughly than before. I noticed, too, that as he stood on point he would roll his eyes in my direction, as if to invite me to complete the task we were working on together. This silent communication was better than a whistle or a shouted command, for it went both ways.

Speck had been staunch for several weeks, as if he had finally accepted that only I could kill the bird, though I didn't do so as often as we would have liked. When I raised the over-and-under for practice and swung on an imaginary pheasant, he danced around the place the bird would have fallen, showing that he understood what followed from the raising of the gun and, by extension, why it might be a good idea to keep me in sight.

That Saturday at Clarence's farm, Speck and I did not achieve the hard-won technical perfection exhibited in field trials by dog and handler alike, but we continued to achieve what I had been hoping for—a tacit understanding between us. When hunting had been a struggle, it was as though Speck had been dreaming on his own, without taking me along into his fantastic inner world. What happened when we hunted together, I thought, was that I came to experience the same dream that he was dreaming, my obliviousness becoming the same as his, his trance becoming no different from mine.

To lose myself in this way was one of the most important reasons why I hunted, and maybe that was because, in loud and frantic America, life had increasingly come to seem like an endless series of distractions from the things that mattered. In this context, being able to escape into one's own world no longer meant being distracted in the most profound manner possible; it meant getting the chance to concentrate, for once, on something that was more than just a dazzling surface or a fleeting moment in time, on something that went all the way down. And hunting with Speck did just that.

On Sunday afternoon, Jim and Clarence took a short break while John and I and Speck walked a wide ribbon of knee-high grass growing on the fenced margin of a soybean field, a spot Jim had dubbed the Meander. There were sloughs at either end, one dry and one thick with cattails in shallow water. As we were starting out, Speck pointed in the dry slough and there followed a mass eruption of roosters, two of which I killed with snap shots as they climbed sharply to the front. A short time later, Speck did something I had read about but never witnessed: he chased a running bird for a time, then sprinted out of the grass and made a circle through the soybeans before returning to the cover we had been walking, trapping the bird between the gun and his intense point. I doubted that a training program could have taught a bird dog to do this; a few more days of hunting wild birds had helped Speck to teach himself. I flushed the rooster and killed it cleanly just as its flight path crossed lines with the top strand of the fence, making three birds in all, the legal limit.

That night we found that the Alaskan giant had gone home.

On Monday morning we awoke, turned on the radio, and got a high wind advisory that clocked at sixty miles an hour the screaming gusts we had been hearing all night. Inside our room it was warm, comfortable, and, because our hosts were storing their Thanksgiving and Christmas decorations on the mantles, rather cozy. When I took Speck outside, the wind stung my eyes, took my breath away, and sent a heavy shovel sliding down the driveway after us. The air temperature was in the low twenties, making for a rare cold day in what had been one of the warmest autumns in memory because—the weathermen repeated—of La Niña events.

As we dressed for one final hunt at the farm, pulling on heavy coats and duck-hunting gloves, I could sense a shared unwillingness to go out in such punishing weather as well as a slightly disappointed recognition that the farm hunt was coming to an end. The evening before, Clarence had returned to his home in a town to the north. The weekend was over. We had killed plenty of birds already, and we had settled up with and said goodbye to our hosts after the patriarch, a white-haired Irish-American show-cattle breeder, had completed a lengthy monologue to which Jim had patiently listened.

At the Dugout, Jim killed one bird over Heidi's point, but no one else had taken a promising shot when my brother suggested we hunt a series of nearby shelterbelts. The wind would batter us as we traversed a long, flat field broken up by the shelterbelts, but the birds would be hunkered down in the relatively thick cover.

Our strategy was part drive, part chase. Jim would block each of the shelterbelts, while John and I would follow Speck.

In the first patch of grass, Speck made game but the birds sprinted away from him. In the second he began to favor John's side of the field. I watched the two of them hunting together and the sight elated me.

I knew that John experienced his time afield with the double perspective the best bird hunters adopt, living the moment not only for itself but as a remembrance deferred. Perhaps these moments would be the ones he would remember while sitting at his desk in the office he had adorned with hunting prints and framed photographs of Remington, the bird dog he had taken on countless hunts between classes at Dartmouth College after he had left home some fifteen years before.

We had covered half the field when the rooster Speck had been chasing flew from the grass and John killed it cleanly. This shot inaugurated a wild few minutes during which numerous roosters fell to our guns. Then there was another lull as we continued to advance across the field. Eventually, three more birds flushed out of range ahead of me. I watched as they reached the tops of the trees in front of us, where the shifting wind forced them into a sweeping flight to the east. Soon Speck pinned one of these roosters in thick grass, and I killed it with a shot that seemed involuntary.

I collected the pheasant from Speck, who seemed to be grinning at me, the way a person might, and we reached the end of the field, where my brother and my uncle were standing out in the roaring wind with their hands full of roosters.

Speck and Heidi, Jim and Clarence, John, and me:
We got our birds.

EPILOGUE

Upward, from unimagined coverts, fly.
—Wallace Stevens, "Blanche McCarthy"

As the season stretched on, first Jim and then John went home. The weather was still fine the December day I closed up the Clear Lake cottage for the winter and Speck and I took to the road again, heading west one last time before we would have to complete the circle we had begun to trace out nearly three months before.

When I think about those last days, it seems that Speck and I were always in the pale grass out in the sunshine, chasing a running bird we couldn't see through public land that was open to the horizon, as if we would never reach a fence that could turn us back. Absorbed by the chase, by our longing for birds and by the things we did on behalf of that longing, we began to forget we existed except to hunt, and we seemed for a time to pass out of the waking world.

Speck floated through the grass without effort,

moving fast but gracefully, putting more and more space between us until he had reached the line we had drawn together in the process of working out a comfortable range.

That had not been a matter simply of training regimes, whistles, and hand signals delivered at just the right moment. It had something to do with teaching and direction on my part, but there was more to it than that. It was also a matter of hunting together, with an oblivious disregard for whatever else was going on around us, for days, weeks, and months at a time.

On our last day, after Speck pointed and retrieved a grasslands prairie chicken, I turned him loose and watched him run across the unbounded territory we had come to see as our own. Soon he was out of sight, and although I kept my eyes fixed on the horizon, there was no way to tell where he had gone. With the open shotgun resting on my shoulder, I climbed the tallest hill I could find and, from the flat crest, waited for a sign that he was still out there.

The air was cold, the light thin and clear. Gusts of wind began to strike the crest from above, driving shallow impressions through the bleached grass. The winter that had been so slow to announce itself appeared finally to be on the way. Elsewhere, I imagined, bird dogs were daydreaming on kitchen floors, safely contained within silent houses outside of Minneapolis or Chicago or, even, Arlington, Virginia.

I knew I needed to reach Interstate 90 before the sun set and before snow, perhaps, began to fall, but nothing other than grass was moving in the draws, and the hillsides, too, were empty. I could only wonder about all the places I couldn't see.

I glanced down at the whistle I was holding now between my numb fingers, trying to think if it would do any good, or if the time of its usefulness had entirely passed. And Speck was there when I raised my head. He was so far off that he seemed to be barely moving, but I could tell that he was sprinting into the wind, that he was running hard in my direction, as though it felt good to find me, and to be found.

I understood, finally, that every now and then I would lose Speck when we hunted; nothing could have been more clear. But I had faith that he would eventually find his way back, as he had done on this last day of our trip and so many times before.

My beloved puppy Huckleberry was gone, of course, and so was Remington, but here was Speck, returning again. He trotted across the flat crest to meet me. I offered a drink of water, but he did not need it. I released him down the hillside and loaded the shotgun. I closed the action and walked after him, the wind at my back.

Three months ago I had imagined that a calamity would overtake us. I had been more than anxious or concerned; I had been afraid. Now I knew that Speck was with me. I understood that, even when he raced out of sight, we were hunting together all the time.